MURDEROUS BOLTON

Steve Fielding is Bolton born and bred. Educated at Bolton County Grammar School, he worked as an engineer before opting for a career as a musician, which has seen him playing shows throughout Britain and in several European countries.

This is his third book. He is the author of "The Hangman's Record" and is one of the country's leading authorities on historical crime and punishment.

He lives in Bolton, working full-time as a writer, and can be seen playing in a band in pubs and clubs around the area.

OTHER TITLES BY STEVE FIELDING:

The Hangman's Record (Volume one).
Published by Chancery House Press, Beckenham, Kent.
June 1994.
ISBN 0 900246 65 0

Lancashire Murder Casebook.
Published by Countryside Books, Newbury, Berkshire.
October 1994.
ISBN 1 853063 25 8

MURDEROUS BOLTON

BY

STEVE FIELDING

OWL
BOOKS

First published November 1994,
by
Owl Books,
P.O. Box 60,
Wigan,
WN1 2QB.

ISBN 1 873888 75 9

Designed and typeset by Coveropen Ltd., Tel: (0524) 425478

Printed and bound in Great Britain.

CONTENTS

ACKNOWLEDGEMENTS

I would like to thank several people who have helped me in compiling this book. First and foremost to Lisa Moore who has helped in every stage; from the researching of cases, through to the proof reading and taking of photographs.

As usual the staff in the Archives and Local Studies Department at Bolton Library have been a great help, as have the staff at Farnworth Library.

I would like to thank the many people who contributed material , in particular Mrs. Marjory Houlihan who generously loaned me material from her own research.

Thanks also to the *Bolton Evening News* who kindly allowed me to reproduce some of the archive illustrations, and to Craig Rice for the front cover design.

Whilst I have made every endeavour to trace the copyright owners on some of the illustrations, some have proved difficult to locate and I therefore apologise in advance if I have unwittingly infringed any copyright.

Opposite: Map of Bolton town centre, dated 1824.

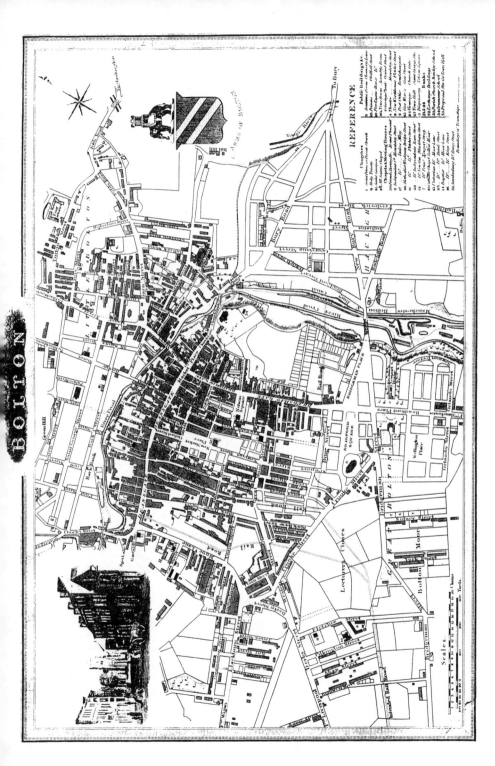

BOLTON

INTRODUCTION

There are two main books that anyone interested in the history of Bolton must read: James Clegg's 'Annals of Bolton' and James Scoles's 'History of Bolton'. Unfortunately both date back from the last century, being published in 1888 and 1892 respectively, and although each make reference to the darker side of Bolton's past, neither contains more than a sentence or two on the various crimes.

It is with this thought in mind that I began this book. There has never before been compiled a collection of Bolton murder cases (with the exception of the odd series of newspaper features), and so considering Bolton's long association with both the murderer and the hangman this long overdue collection of stories has been written to fill a conspicuous gap.

One of the earliest recorded Boltonians to end his life on the scaffold was Thomas Pilkington — a family name long associated with the town — who paid with his life for his allegiance to the defeated Richard the third, when he was beheaded at Leicester in 1485.

Few towns suffered more than Bolton in the Civil War and a legacy of those dark days remains on the corner of Churchgate opposite the Swan Hotel. On Wednesday October 15th, 1651, James Stanley, the seventh Earl of Derby, was beheaded at the Market Cross for his active support of the Royal Cause. The monument that still stands today was erected in memory of the event.

A few decades earlier, the town had played the unwelcome host to a number of witchcraft trials, and as a result several of those suspected and convicted of being witches were either burned at the stake or hanged on a gibbet. Being burned at the stake was a fate that was also bestowed upon one Mary Hilton after being convicted of poisoning her husband at Middle Hulton in 1772.

Eight years later the first cotton mill was erected in the town on King's Street, Burnden. It's founder was James Thwaites (or Tweats). The bleaching of the cotton was done in the open air and the offence of stealing cloth – croft breaking – was punishable by death.

In 1786, James Holland was convicted of stealing thirty yards of cotton (valued at three pounds) from Mr. Thwaites' mill. Holland was hanged at Lancaster and afterwards his body brought back to Bolton and suspended on the gibbet erected on Deane Moor near Sunning Hill on what was known for a time as Gallows Hill. Ten years later the body of Samuel Longworth was displayed on the same spot. Longworth's crime – murder of William Horrox at Deane – is the starting point for this chronicle of Bolton killers.

In 1812, the country, and in particular the industrial regions, were gripped with a number of riots, disturbances and political unrest as workers under the guidance of General Ludd rebelled against the progress of technology at the expense of manpower. A Westhoughton factory belonging to Messrs Wroe and Duncough was

Bolton's oldest Pub 'Ye Olde Man & Scythe'

burnt to the ground by 'Luddites' protesting at their new practice of 'weaving by steam'.

At Lancaster Assizes in June, four of those arrested; Job Fletcher (34), of Atherton, Thomas Kerfoot (26), of Westhoughton, James Smith (31), of Bolton and fourteen year old Abraham Charlton were convicted and hanged. A cart was sent to Lancaster asking for the return of their bodies after execution so that they could be given a Christian burial in their home towns, but it was sent back empty, the request refused.

Throughout the rest of the 19th century Bolton's link with murder was frequently in the headlines. A selection of the more interesting cases follows this introduction.

The town of Bolton was also the home to a number of killers whose methods were authorised by the state. Between 1884 and 1905 the name of Billington appeared on the list of the country's hangmen. The first of that family to hold this mantle was James Billington. Born in Bolton in 1847, Billington was a twice married father of six who worked as a piecer in a local mill where he earned the curious nickname of 'Jimmy Armhole'. At various other times he was also a miner, a wrestler and a pub singer.

During the early 1880s the whole rigmarole of hanging was

James Billington

TWO EXECUTIONS THIS MORNING.

THE SHEFFIELD TRAGEDY.

SCENE IN THE GAOL

Joseph Laycock, who murdered his wife and four children at Sheffield in July last, was hanged this morning at Armley Gaol, Leeds. A man named Billington, of Bolton, was the executioner. Representatives of the press were not admitted.

Another telegram says that Billington is an ex-collier and barber, of Farnworth. He has not before conducted an execution, but performed his task with great celerity. The prisoner fainted on the executioner entering the cell, but restoratives were immediately applied.

The following letter had been received from the Home Office by a gentleman in Leeds who wrote to the Home Secretary urging that there were circumstances connected with Joseph Laycock's crime which rendered it essential that an authoritative medical inquiry should be made into the question of his responsibility at the time of the murder :—" Whitehall, 23rd August, 1884. Sir,— With reference to your application in behalf of Joseph Laycock, I am directed by the Secretary of State to acquaint you after full and careful consideration of the circumstances, and after appointing two medical men, under the provisions of 27 and 28 Vic., cap. 29, sec. 2, to make special inquiry into the state of mind of this man, he has been unable to find sufficient grounds to justify him in advising interference with the due course of the law.—I am, sir, your obedient servant, " A. F. O. LIDDELL."

Newspaper report of Billington's first execution, 1884.

being revised as theories were put into practise trying to devise methods of imparting instant death by a broken neck, as opposed to slow painful strangulation. Billington, now working as a barber in Farnworth, practised his chosen methods in the back yard of his shop on Market Street using dummies and weights, and after securing an interview with the Governor of Leeds Prison in the spring of 1884, he was appointed as the official executioner for the County of Yorkshire.

Upon the retirement of the country's chief executioner, James Berry, in 1892, Billington was promoted to the top of the list. During the late 1890s he was often assisted by Boltonian William Wilkinson, an insurance salesman from Blackburn Road, who changed his name to Warbrick when he learned that his parents weren't married.

In 1897 the first of Billington's three sons graduated onto the list of hangmen. Thomas, his eldest son, was an assistant until his own death in 1902 at a tragically early age, coming just a matter of weeks after his father passed away. Thomas had been joined by second son William in 1898 and when Thomas died a third son, Jack, took his place.

William retired in 1904 and was later sent to prison for failing to pay maintenance money to his wife. Jack carried on as the last of the Billington hangmen until his own untimely death in 1905. He had suffered an unfortunate incident while carrying out an execution at Leeds prison where he fell through the trapdoor whilst rigging the scaffold. He suffered internal bleeding and although he was able to carry out the sentence as planned, he returned home and was confined to bed. Six weeks later, at the age of twenty nine, he died from dropsy, brought on by the fall.

There have, of course, been many other local murderers and hangmen in the 20th century, and a further selection of these cases will be recorded in the follow up volume of *Murderous Bolton*, which will chronicle Bolton murders from more modern times.

Steve Fielding
1994

CHAPTER 1

Murder on Deane Moor

IT was shortly after 7-30pm, October 27th, 1796, as eighteen year old William Horrox junior returned to his home near Deane Church, carrying with him five guineas, some small change and provisions of tea, bread and candles. As he made his way up the main highway out of town, approaching what is now Deane Church lane he was attacked, robbed, and then beaten to death.

Two local surgeons, Dr Barlow and Dr Graham, examined the body of the youngster and found that he had received two blows to the back of the head: one to the back of the skull, the other to the temple. It was the latter which had proved fatal. William's body was later buried in the church that faced his family home.

The killer had fled in the darkness and was at large for several weeks prompting the local newspaper to report:

*"We hope that the law, justice, judgement and vengeance
will soon overtake him and that he may suffer a death in
some respects equal to the magnitude of his crime".*

When the murderer's identity was finally revealed, it came from a most unusual source.

Several weeks after the terrible crime, Samuel Longworth and his wife were quarrelling in the garden of their cottage at Dicconson Lane, Aspull, near Wigan, and during the row he

Deane Church. William Horrox's home overloooked this medieval landmark.

struck her across the face. As she fell to the ground and he moved in closer, she demanded to know if he was going to do the same to her as he done to that poor fellow at Deane.

A neighbour overheard these remarks and after pondering over them for a while, he reported it to the Parish Constable. Longworth's wife was later questioned and as a result, two days before Christmas, her husband was arrested and charged with wilful murder.

Samuel Longworth was tried for his crime at Lancaster Assizes in April 1797 and the jury convicted him on the evidence before them. He was sentenced to be hanged at Lancaster Castle and afterwards his body be removed to Deane and suspended in Gibbets.

The execution was carried out as planned and Longworth was gibbetted near what later became Willows Lane. His body hung in the wind and rain for several weeks during which time it was pecked at by the crows until an order was given allowing the remains to be buried.

POSTSCRIPT: In 1887, workmen excavating foundations for houses in the Willows Lane area, unearthed the remains of Samuel Longworth. They were later re-interred in a local churchyard.

Gibbetting

A common form of displaying a criminal's body after execution. The felon was first dispatched on a normal scaffold. The body was then taken down, encased in iron bands, and then hung on the gibbet. Occasionally if the body was to be suspended for a long time, the body was coated in either pitch or resin to prevent decomposition, but more often than not the corpse was suspended untreated. Gibbets were usually situated on the main road into town where they were to act as a determent for any would be criminals. The body was normally removed after the birds had feasted upon it. It was abolished in England in 1834.

CHAPTER 2

A Poisoned Pudding

TO the guests arriving at the Nailers Green Hotel, Tottington, the 'Select Vestry and Parish Officers Dinner' of roast beef, legs of mutton, cheeses and plum puddings had several licking their lips in anticipation. It was the early evening, Friday, September 11th, 1829, and the fourteen guests comprised solely of members of the St Annes Church Parish Select Vestry, (the Select Vestry being the forerunner of the modern district council), and for many weeks members had contributed, by way of fines for missing meetings etc, towards the spread which had long been a annual event.

The members of the Vestry carried a high level of responsibility which included deciding on hand-outs for the poorer end of the community. As the welfare payments were at the discretion of the council, several members became the target of criticism from certain members of the community who accused them of being unfairly selective in making the awards.

Those sitting down to the meal included the local vicar, the choir-master, several wealthy mill-owners, and the governor of the local workhouse, which was at that time near Holcombe Brook.

The atmosphere at the dining table was rich with laughter especially when one of the more portly gentlemen, James Booth, a bleacher from Woolford, helped himself to extra helpings of the plum pudding. As the others settled back with a brandy and cigar, Booth announced that he suddenly felt ill and hurried from the room accompanied by a roar of laughter.

"Serves the greedy devil right" laughed one of the men, but no sooner had he spoken than he too was out of his seat heading for the door. Within the next few minutes one after the other dashed from the room to be sick in the yard outside. One man who didn't make the journey from the table was James Livesey, the workhouse governor. He had arrived at the Hotel complaining of feeling unwell but telling his fellow guests that as he had paid for the food he may as well try to enjoy what he could. His fellow guests couldn't help noticing however, that he merely picked at the food and enjoyed neither the sweet nor the cheese-board.

Poor James Booth was wretching so badly that at 6pm he decided to go home. He faced a three mile walk home not helped by him stumbling and vomiting every hundred or so yards. Accompanied by a neighbour James Green, the journey took him close on two hours and when he arrived home he was in such a state that his wife wasted no time in hurrying to fetch a doctor. Booth's condition deteriorated through the night and by noon he had died.

At the inquest held later that day, doctors were baffled as to the cause of death of the previously healthy man. They suspected that death may have been caused by using dirty brass or copper instruments in the preparation of the food. It was not unknown for a poisonous crystallisation - verdigris - to contaminate the food, but a check of the kitchen quickly ruled out this theory. It was when they closely examined the cloth used to steam the plum pudding that they found the cause. Trapped in a fold on the cloth were traces of arsenic.

Police now knew the cause of death but how had it got there? An inquest was held at the Spread Eagle Hotel at Bury where evidence was heard by a Bury druggist who admitted selling arsenic to two strangers shortly before the death of Mr

Booth. The men had claimed the arsenic was for William Kay, the landlord of the Nailers Green Hotel who was having problems with mice in the kitchen. Kay said he had authorised no such errand.

The landlord and his wife gave evidence at the inquest, although the coroner went to great lengths to assure them that they weren't on trial. The couple had been running the hotel for almost twenty years and Mrs Kay told the court she had made the food herself in the out-house at the hotel.

It was when the coroner asked if anyone other than the staff, who had all been able to satisfy police of their innocence, had access to the food, that what may have happened became clearer.

Mrs Kay told him that a large open fire was kept burning in the out-house and it was usual for customers to use it to light their pipes. Mrs Kay, however, was adamant that nobody had used the out-house whilst she was preparing the meal.

The inquest ended with the coroner ruling that James Booth had been unlawfully killed by arsenic poisoning, by person or persons unknown.

The surviving members of the vestry clubbed together and offered a reward of one hundred pounds for information leading to the conviction of the poisoner but the money was never claimed and the mystery was never solved. At the inquest it was soon clear that they had all been the target for the planned poisoning, although only Mr Booth had consumed enough of the poisoned pudding for it to be fatal.

POSTSCRIPT: So who did kill James Booth? Although the druggist claimed that he had sold arsenic to two men who said it was destined for Mr Kay at the hotel, there is no proof that this was the case, and indeed what motive would the landlord have for poisoning his more affluent customers. Descriptions of the two men didn't match those of any regular customers and it was unlikely that a stranger would know the plan of the hotel and gain access to the food.

A newspaper article written on the case many years later claimed that the likely poisoner was known to the Governor of the workhouse. Livesey was the only one who didn't eat much that night, he had, remember, complained of feeling unwell. Did he know that perhaps some of the poor folk at the workhouse had spiked the food due to some grievance over welfare payments?

Was Livesey covering for the killer? Could a man of such high standing in the community, who was, after all, a colleague and friend of the murdered man, sit tight and let someone get away with a callous murder. Unlikely? Perhaps, but then we'll never know!

CHAPTER 3

Resurrectionists
at Rose-hill?

THROUGHOUT the country, from a period beginning sometime around 1750, freshly buried corpses mysteriously began to disappear. It later transpired that these bodies ended up in the hands of surgeons and those studying anatomy, used for practice and the further study of human science. Despite the sacriligious practice the methods and reasons for it were primarily to aid study and were looked upon with gratitude by medical students and Fellows of the Royal Society.

The practice though had a down side. Soon the demand for freshly buried corpses outweighed the supply and some of the more enterprising of the 'Resurrectionists' as they had been dubbed, found that if newly dead bodies weren't readily available they would have to supply their own and thus embarked on killing sprees.

The most famous of these 'Resurrectionists' were two Scots, William Burke and William Hare, whose grisly reign ended when they fell out and tried to blame each other for their crimes. Hare turned King's evidence and disappeared, Burke was hanged in front of a large crowd at Edinburgh in January 1829.

In that same year two young boys out playing in a tunnel under the high road at Rose-Hill, stumbled across the body of a

Contemporary drawing of "Resurrectionists" at work.

man tied up in a sack. The local constable was at a loss as to how it had gotten there, and at the coroners inquest no evidence could be found to suggest the cause of death. Surgeons at the inquest argued for and against the theory that the body was the work of resurrectionists and destined for the local hospital. The final verdict on the mystery body was: "deceased found dead in a tunnel, but how he came to be there, there is no evidence to show".

The identity of the body remained a mystery until the end of July 1831, over two years later, when Mrs Elizabeth Hooper, a respectable Manchester housekeeper, called to speak to the minister of Trinity Church.

In searching for her husband, she had been making enquiries amongst travellers in his profession (he was a saddle-maker), and spoke to a man named Brewer who told her he had been murdered near Bolton.

She had last seen her husband and father of two, John

Hooper, on the May 16th, 1829 when he had set out to travel on business to Knutsford. He was employed at the time by Walter Paulton, a Bolton saddler. No-one had seen him since the afternoon he set out towards Knutsford.

Brewer was questioned by one of her friends and told a different story; this time he claimed he had heard that Hooper had drowned near Bolton. Then she had heard about the gruesome discovery at Rosehill.

Confident that she could identify if the corpse was that of her husband she described him to the minister. "Broad set, with a prominent forehead, black hair and one of his upper front teeth missing.

A warrant was obtained and the coffin disinterred. It was partly filled with water and the body badly decomposed but the distinguishing marks described by Mrs Hooper were all present. The corpse was formally identified and re-interred in the Trinity churchyard.

A search was made for Brewer who had disappeared from his job about a month earlier. It was learned that he had tried to emigrate to America but as his wife was pregnant the ship's Captain refused her permission to board and rather than desert her he stayed in England. He was described by those who knew him as a good family man and a hard worker.

Brewer was arrested in Staffordshire and brought to Bolton where he was remanded on bail. It appears that while in Bolton, Brewer disappeared after being released on sureties of twenty pounds, which never materialised, and that no charges were ever brought against him.

POSTSCRIPT: So who did kill John Hooper? In January 1830 a man named Hannah was convicted at Lancaster Assizes for having in his possession the dead body of one George Dean who had recently been laid to rest in Bolton parish church graveyard. When he was arrested papers found on him showed that he had made over eighty pounds from the sale of

Dr. Knox

seven bodies which he had sent to Edinburgh for the attention of the infamous Dr Knox, who was closely associated with Burke and Hare.

Was John Hooper destined for Edinburgh? Hannah never admitted the murder nor was he charged with that crime when he stood trial at Lancaster. He was convicted of being in possession of stolen corpses and sentenced to six months imprisonment.

CHAPTER 4

The Body in the River Croal

THE peace of the early hours of Sunday, July 29th, 1832, was shattered by a piercing scream. John Lee, a resident living in the Spawfields district of Little Bolton, heard the noise and went to investigate. In the darkness he saw a crowd of perhaps half a dozen men and a solitary female, who appeared, from the tone of her voice, to be in distress and evidently being taken somewhere against her will.

Grabbing his hat and coat, Lee turned to his wife and said that he would follow and see what they were up to. Keeping to the shadows, he watched them walk down a footpath leading towards Gilnow then make for a field known as Bamber's Pasture, where they stopped.

The woman began to shout and scream as she was thrown to the ground, and it appeared from her screaming that one of the men was forcing himself on her. Lee walked into the field and found one of the men struggling on the ground with the woman.

"It's a burning shame to use any woman in that manner", he protested. The men replied that they weren't hurting her and had no intention of doing so. "Why did she scream so", Lee went on, and as he spoke he recognised the man grappling on the floor.

Lee realised that he was powerless to do anything, and not only that, but he was also in danger of being beaten up himself if he stayed around, so he decided to retreat and seek assistance for the unfortunate woman.

Returning home he met up with his brother and another friend and they were soon joined by two neighbours. Lee told them what he had seen and they hurried back to the field. Approaching the pasture they saw a group of five men but there was no sign of the woman. The two groups passed on the path, with Lee and his friends walking down towards the gas works. They walked back up Spaw Lane and as they approached Garside barracks the two gangs met up again.

One of the gang Lee had earlier seen with the woman turned and spoke to him: "What have you done with the woman?". Lee replied "What have you done with her!" One of the gang then admitted that the last time they saw her she was with Jem Johnson, then added "It would be a serious thing if she got into the brook and drowned".

Both groups then set out towards Moor Lane where they split up. Lee's friends between them recognised four of the five in the gang and had heard one of the men say that the missing man was Jem Johnson.

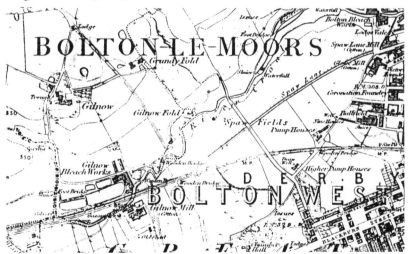

Map showing the Spaw Field area of Bolton, 1830's.

On Monday morning William Appleyard called to see his brother's widow, thirty two year old Alice Berry, who lived with her two children on back Ormrod street. She had been missing since Saturday night when after an evening out with relatives, she had arrived home at 11pm, checked that the children were asleep, and then popped out for a drink at 'The Volunteer'. She left there in the company of a friend and her husband and headed for 'The Flag' two hundred yards from her home. She had not been seen since.

Appleyard along with his friends Thomas Foster and William Banks, checked the surrounding area for his sister- in-law, and eventually made a gruesome discovery as they searched near Coulthard's bleach works. Lying face down in the adjoining River Croal was the body of Alice Berry.

Word soon reached Lee that a body had been found in the river and he wasted no time in contacting the local Parish Constable, Thomas Barrett, with his information. The men identified by Lee and his friends were quickly rounded up and by late afternoon had been taken into custody.

Dr Heap, the local surgeon, examined the body and found no external bruises severe enough to have caused death, although he did note the presence of marks on her arms, elbows and shins, as if she had been dragged down a gravel path.

On Wednesday, February 1st, six men stood before the coroner's court held at The Three Tuns on Bridge Street. It was held here and not at the usual venue, The White Lion Inn, Deansgate, because it was feared a big crowd might congregate so angry was the local feelings against the men.

Those indicted were named as: James 'Jem' Johnson (40), a spinner; William Coffey (26) married with two children, a weaver; William Hardman (18), clogger; Benjamin Brown (19), moulder; Roger Kearsley (21), carder; Richard Bolton (19), a brick setter.

After hearing evidence by John Lee, which was corroborated by several independent witnesses who had seen the terrified woman being dragged through the streets, the court ended by remanding the six to appear at Lancaster Assizes on a charge of manslaughter.

The men stood trial in the spring. Evidence was given by Dr Heap who had to admit that the woman could have fainted or fallen into the river and drowned. When the Judge came to sum up the case, he guided the jury that there was great doubt as to how the woman met her death but left it up to them to decide whether they believed them guilty of manslaughter or even murder. They took only a short time to acquit the prisoners on the charge of manslaughter. They were then re-leased pending further charges.

On Wednesday, August 15th, 1832, the six found them-selves back in the dock at Lancaster, but this time they were to be tried only on a the charge of assault with intent to commit rape. In summing up, the counsel highlighted the need for a heavily populated town such as Bolton to have a proper police force and not have to rely on the parish force, although he did later commend Constable Barrett on his good work.

The six were found guilty of the revised charges and were each sentenced to two years imprisonment with hard labour, with the exception of Hardman, who had informed on the others after being arrested. He received one year in prison with hard labour.

The Development of Bolton Police Force

At the time of the assault on Alice Berry, Bolton was policed by what was known as a watch. Parish Constable Thomas Barrett was elected to his position and usually had to rely on informers and back-handers to arrest thieves. Despite the prosecution counsel's calling for a town police force, Bolton did not have a recognised police force until 1839.

More information on the history of the Bolton Force can be found in the excellent book "Duty Bound" by RJ Goslin (1970).

CHAPTER 5

The Bradshawgate Gang

I T'S probably no surprise for anyone to discover that after dark, the streets of Bolton, or indeed any major town centre, aren't always a safe place. All too frequently newspapers carry stories of people being assaulted or beaten up as they innocently make their way home from some pub, club, restaurant or cinema but anyone who thinks this is a new phenomena may be a little surprised to read that these same Bolton town centre streets have a long history of violence.

Over a hundred and fifty years ago certain parts of the town were almost a no-go area for decent citizens, as gangs of drink sodden thugs would drift from the shadows waylaying and robbing any easy targets that strayed past. Amongst the worst of these were the Bradshawgate Gang, a feared mob who terrorised, as their name implied, that area of the town.

It was in the early hours of Sunday, September 9th, 1832, as two men made their way home after attending a function in the town. Twenty four year old John Fray and his brother-in-law John Paton were passing Nelson Square when they heard shouts for help. It was a woman's voice and the cry for help was repeated, this time with the words 'murder' tagged on the end.

The Pack Horse, Nelson Square, Bradshawgate.

Fray hurried over and saw a woman being kicked by a man. He shouted for him to stop and added that that was no way for a man to behave. The attacker told him to mind his business and there was an angry exchange of words. Fray realising now that the attacker and his victim were at most having a lovers tiff, strode off to rejoin Paton.

The two carried on walking but hadn't gone more than a few paces when the attacker whistled loudly and several men approached. The two men, fearing a beating took to their heals. The first attacker threw his coat to one of those who had joined him, and set off in pursuit of the fleeing men.

Paton managed to escape around the corner but Fray was quickly outpaced and brought to the ground with a crashing tackle. Moments later the others caught up and as Paton watched helplessly from a safe distance, the gang proceeded to kick the terrified man into unconsciousness. One man in particular was acting in an excessively violent manner. Despite it being obvious that the victim was unconscious, he took a few steps back, and then ran at great speed towards his stricken prey, lashing out hard at the man's head with his heavy boots. It was later found that this blow to the head proved fatal.

Constable Thomas Barrett and his deputy John Rollinson were quickly informed of the murder having strong suspicions of those they thought responsible the two officers raided a boarding house in a less salubrious area of the town where they took a number of men in for questioning.

Charles Lomax (20), James Aspinall (21), and William Crossley (21), along with Mary Crompton were charged with causing the felonious death of John Fray on September 9th.

An inquest was held at the Pack Horse on Tuesday morning, where the events of the previous Sunday were told to the court. The coroner heard how Lomax, recently discharged from Salford Prison after serving a sentence for highway robbery, began a drunken quarrel with Mary Crompton his girlfriend. Miss Crompton was a woman of questionable virtue who because of short stature went under the unflattering nickname of 'Humpy'! During the quarrel she called Lomax an abusive name and he replied by slapping her across the face. She cried out in pain and it was this cry that had alerted Fray and Paton.

The inquest ended with Miss Crompton being acquitted on the charge of causing the death of Fray; the three men were remanded to face trial at Lancaster Assizes. At a separate hearing later that day Mary Crompton was committed to Salford's New Bailey prison for one month charged with being a vagrant and common prostitute.

At Lancaster Assizes in March 1833, the three men were arraigned on a coroners inquisition of the wilful murder of John Fray. The Grand Jury ignored the bill for murder and acquitted them of the capital charge, instead opting to try the prisoners on the lesser charge of aggravated manslaughter.

They appeared before Mr Justice Alderson and the summary of events leading up to the death of John Fray were heard. At one stage the Judge interrupted proceedings and asked if there were no watchmen in Bolton. Learning that there were no other law enforcers other than two constables and a Borough-breeve, Mr Justice Alderstone recommended that the town acquired itself a larger police force.

It was only a relatively short trial and ended with verdicts of guilty as charged against the three men. The judge then made a scathing address about the state of certain areas of the town and implementing recommendations that the illegal drinking houses and brothels were cleaned up as a matter of urgency.

Addressing the prisoners, the judge then proceeded to pass sentence:

> *'You, James Aspinall, took a most brutal part in the transaction. To your brutality the unfortunate man Fray owes his death. You saw him struggling on the ground and like a coward took a deliberate run and kicked him in the head. Your offence merits the upmost severity of the law. It is lamentable that in this country there are persons so base as to attack in numbers, offending men with the greatest disregard to human life.*
>
> *(Here Aspinall hung his head in shame)*
>
> *Well may you hide your face from the just indignation of your country. You, Charles Lomax, first strike a woman and it is not to be wondered at, that the man who was coward enough to abuse a female should call his comrades to his assistance in order to combat a man. You, William Crossley, stand in the same situation as Lomax; you kicked the deceased and was present assisting your companions. I sentence you Aspinall to transportation from these shores for the rest of your natural life. Lomax, you shall be transported from this Island for the period of fourteen years, and you Crossley shall likewise be transported, but in your case the period shall be seven years.*

Transportation

A former punishment first implemented towards the end of the 17th century. It involved sending convicted felons to other parts of the Empire either for life or shorter periods, depending on the severity of the offence. Initially convicts were shipped to America but this practice was stopped after America gained it's independence. From thence they were shipped to Australia. Convicts were transported in cramped ships in terrible conditions, and many convicts perished on the journey. The practice was stopped by the British Government in 1857, by which time many thousands had been transported. France also used transportation as a punishment, and in their case it continued until 1938.

CHAPTER 6

The Despicable Betty Eccles

T WENTY eight year old Harry Eccles had barely recovered from the shock of losing his wife in childbirth, at a tragically early age, when he began a relationship with his close neighbour Betty Haslam. At ten years older than Harry, Betty was also recovering from the bereavement of two of her children and as they grew closer she became a great help, looking after his young children while he was forced to work away in Manchester. His job meant he had to stay the week in Manchester, returning to his home at Turner Bridge after his shift on Sunday morning, leaving for work barely twenty-four hours later.

The appearance of Betty meant the children were better cared for and his happiness was compounded when she accepted his proposal of marriage, and in January 1841 they became man and wife.

Life at last seemed to be treating Harry well, but within eighteen months tragedy again courted the Eccles family. Returning home from work in June 1842, he was shocked to find that little Billy Heywood, a neighbours son, who Betty minded during the day, had collapsed and died after suffering a fit.

Three months later, the wings of death again cloaked the house as Betty's eldest daughter Alice died while he was at work. Harry wasn't informed of the passing of the hitherto healthy child and when he returned home at the end of his weeks work, Alice was already in her grave. She had also suffered a fit.

The old adage that bad news comes in threes, was proved right when Harry's eldest son Bill passed away a fortnight later. Betty told her husband that the fifteen year old lad, who like his sister had been in previous good health, had died from inflammation, but inflammation of what she didn't elaborate.

Three sudden deaths in such a short time had the neighbour's tongues wagging to such an extent that officers from Bolton borough police visited the house and asked a number of questions. Whilst her husband may have been satisfied with her explanations, the police clearly were not, and asked a local doctor, Joseph Denham, to carry out a post mortem on William Eccles.

Inspector James Harris was placed in charge of the investigation and ordered the bodies to be transferred to the local hospital where after an examination, Denham told him that the stomach and intestines were inflamed, and that his initial diagnosis suggested that the boy had been poisoned. This was confirmed when a more detailed examination later found traces of arsenic.

Harris then decided to exhume Alice's body and despite her coffin already showing considerable signs of decomposition, the stomach was still in reasonable condition and when examined it too contained traces of arsenic. It was perhaps ironic that it was the very presence of arsenic in the stomach prevented it from decomposition.

The coffins of Betty's two children, Nancy and Hannah, who had died before she met Harry Eccles, and the body of the baby Heywood were also exhumed. Traces of arsenic were present in the organs of Nancy but police were unable to be sure in the cases of the other two. Convinced that he was dealing with a mass poisoner, Inspector Harris decided to charge Betty Eccles with murder.

She stood trial at Liverpool Assizes on Tuesday April 4th 1843, and pleaded not guilty. She was only to be charged with the murder of William, but evidence would be heard regarding the deaths of her other children. The evidence against her, particularly from her step children, was damning and the court listened in silence as thirteen year old Richard Eccles told how on the day of his brothers death he was surprised to find that when he arrived home from the mill, William had already been fed and the dishes cleared. William had even boasted that he had been given a pudding, which wasn't offered to the other children. He also claimed that William seemed to have been singled out for particularly brutal treatment from their step-mother. William further earned her wrath when he threatened to tell his father after Betty had returned home one evening very drunk. Betty coldly told the boy that she would shut him up if he uttered a word about this to his father.

The one weakness in the prosecution case was the lack of proof that Betty had administered the poison, although a local chemist testified that they had served her with some poison which she claimed was to kill mice.

The boss at Eden and Thwaites mill where William worked also testified against Betty. He claimed that he had given her a loan to help pay for the funeral of Alice which he agreed to deduct from William's wage. Betty asked and was told that if William should die she would be entitled to fifty shillings, and the conversation was still fresh in his mind when William Eccles died. Betty never collected the money; she was arrested before the factory re-opened for the week.

The police doctor who had examined William told the court that the boy's stomach contained 33/35 grains of the poison, an amount that would have proved fatal within a matter of hours. William had eaten his lunch at two o'clock and by three he had become so ill that he was sent home. Thomas Davenport, a workmate, left the factory an hour later and came across William lying in a ditch, and escorted him home. Betty said she had called on the boy's doctor, Dr Mallet, but he was out on a call so she gave him a tonic and sent him to bed, where he died later that evening.

The defence made the best of a hard case but it was no surprise when the jury needed just forty-five minutes to find Betty Eccles guilty of the wilful murder of her step-son, and she was sentenced to death. She stood silently as the sentence was passed but as she led from the dock she began to scream for mercy.

It had long been a custom in British courts that cold, calculated poisoners were rarely reprieved, and Betty was to be no exception, for at noon on a warm, spring Saturday, May 6th, 1843, she was hanged outside Liverpool's Kirkdale prison. She was joined on the drop by Wilmot Buckley who had killed his wife at St Helens. Placing his ropes around the prisoners's necks, executioner Calcraft pushed the lever and the trap fell. Buckley died at once, but the crowd watched in horror as Betty Eccles struggled hard for several minutes until she died, not from a broken neck, but from painful, slow strangulation.

EXECUTION OF WILMOT BUCKLEY AND BETTY ECCLES AT KIRKDALE.

At twelve o'clock on Saturday Wilmot Buckley, convicted, at the last assizes, of the wilful murder of his wife, at St. Helen's, and Betty Eccles, of the wilful murder, by poison, of her step-son, at Bolton, underwent the extreme sentence of the law at the usual

---

POSTSCRIPT: The true count of Betty Eccles's victims has never been officially recorded. Apart from the deaths of her children both before and after her marriage to Harry Eccles, there was also a number of unexplained, sudden deaths in her past, even her first husband had died suddenly. The final total could even have been in double figures.

36

CHAPTER 7

Fatal Shooting at Garside Barracks

O N one side of Garside street, across from where Hawthorns nightclub stands, once stood an Infantry Barracks. Early maps have the words temporary in brackets but the barracks stood for many years, probably first built to hold troops destined to join Wellington in fighting the French in foreign fields.

In 1833 the barracks were home to the 35th Regiment of Foot, currently standing domicile. One Thursday night, a number of soldiers ventured into Bolton town centre where they began to drink heavily. Being used to action, the routine of drill and musketry practice tried the patience of men who had joined to fight and many found the only way to kill the dreary hours was to become lost in an alcohol induced state. This of course, was contrary to army regulations and any soldier found drunk on duty faced a heavy punishment.

Two weeks earlier thirty year old private John Wilson was brought up on such a charge and as a result was confined to barracks and fined a hefty sum. Wilson was one of many in the regiment who hailed from the local area, being an ex-labourer formerly of Great Bolton. On the following Friday morning,

October 4th, Wilson woke early and left the barracks to meet up with a friend for a drink. Despite it being only 8 o'clock he ordered a large jug of ale and settled down to drink it.

His friend, aware that Wilson was due to go on parade, told him he had better get back to camp, to which Wilson replied "I'll sup this lot first, then I'll be away". Emptying his glass, the soldier got to his feet and stumbled as he tried to regain his balance. He was clearly quite drunk.

Under the command of Lieutenant Ward, the soldiers paraded on the drill square. As Wilson took his place in line he was spoken to by Sergeant Thomas Gordon who noticed at once that he was drunk.

Gordon reported this to Lieutenant Ward who had Wilson

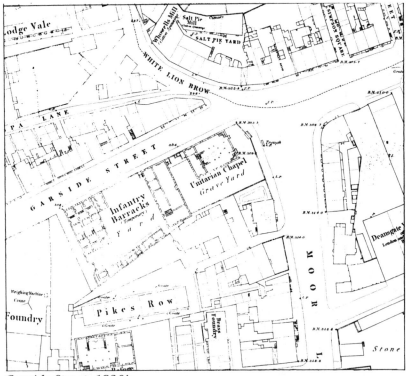

Garside Street, 1830's.

removed from the square under escort and taken to the guard-room. Corporal James Britten was in charge of the escort and as they reach the building, adjacent to the Sergeant-Major's quarters, Wilson turned to his escort: "I suppose I am going to be rammed in the guard house again?" The officer made no reply merely closing the door after Wilson and sliding the bolt.

Private Johnson was pacing in front of the orderly room window when he saw Wilson looking through the bars on the window. He saw the soldier retreat then re-approach with his fire-lock (an early form of rifle), present it to the company drilling on the square, and then fire.

The gun shot attracted the attention of Private Woods who was on duty in the guardroom and he dashed over and wrested the gun from Wilson who was immediately held.

Lieutenant Ward who was addressing the men when the shot rang out, saw two of his men stagger and then one fall to the ground. The ball had struck Private Edmund Martin through the cross-belt and passed through his abdomen. It had then struck the hand of Private James Branston before smashing the musket held by a third soldier.

Private Martin was a forty year old native of Colchester, who had been a soldier for twenty-seven years, having spent much of his time fighting overseas, and had served under Wellington at Waterloo.

Dr Joseph Lomax Heap, the town surgeon, was quickly summoned and he arrived fifteen minutes after the incident to find the soldier in a bad way. The shot had destroyed his liver, and his intestines and bowels protruded from an horrific wound to the stomach. Dr Heap administered a painkiller but the man died from his wounds shortly after noon. Dr Heap had been accompanied to the barracks by Constable Burrows who took the prisoner into police custody, as the matter had now passed from a military matter to a civil one.

On the following morning an inquest was held at the Hen and Chickens on Deansgate before Mr W S Rutter the borough

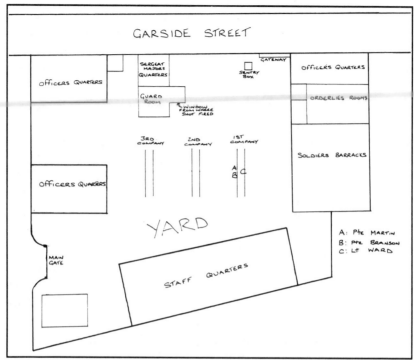

Plan of Garside Barracks.

coroner. Evidence was heard from members of Wilson's company and the inquest closed with Wilson being remanded for trial at Lancaster Assizes charged with the wilful murder of Private Martin. Wilson was taken by stage coach to Lancaster under the guard of Constable Burrows. As the coach left Bolton a large crowd gathered to watch as the soldier was led away. Burrows reported back that his prisoner had bore up well at the outset but by the time the coach had reached Preston he had become overcome with dread and on reaching Lancaster castle a more pitiful sight he could not have witnessed, as Wilson had to be carried to his cell.

The trial opened before Mr Justice Taunton on March 12th, 1834. The calendar of cases for this sitting of the assizes was very heavy and in his opening speech the Judge referred to the various cases and singled out Wilson.

He informed the jury that the prisoner Wilson had made no pre-conceived malice against Edmund Martin. He pointed out the differences between types of intent by citing an example.

"If a man attempts to shoot 'A' against whom he has malice but hits 'B' then it is murder because he showed malice when he fired the gun".

Opening the case, Mr Brandt for the prosecution, said the only question regarding the case is whether Wilson was guilty of murder or manslaughter.

Evidence was heard that Wilson had claimed he had not had any intent when he pulled the trigger and realising at once the tragic consequences of his actions, he had planned to take his own life. Private Woods's intervention prevented him from doing this.

The short trial ended when the jury were asked to consider their verdict. They chose not to retire, instead after a short conference they announced that they found Wilson not guilty of murder but guilty of manslaughter.

Wilson, who had stood almost rigid with terror while waiting for the verdict, went deathly pale and staring up at the sky, began whispering: "Thank you my Lord, Oh Thank you, thank you".

Judge Taunton then addressed the prisoner:

"John Wilson you are acquitted of the foul crime of murder but the jury in finding you guilty of manslaughter have put a most merciful interpretation on the evidence.... The sentence is that you be transported beyond the seas to such a place as His Majesty may direct, for the term of your natural life.

CHAPTER 8

Scotchman's Stump

THE swirling mist that blanketed the vast barren Horwich moorland could scarcely have looked more un-inviting as a young traveller set out alone towards Belmont village.

Twenty year old George Henderson was a native of Annan, Dumfries, and his job as salesman for a firm of Blackburn drapers often meant long hours on the road and as he usually carried sums of money he was constantly at risk from attack.

It was November 9th, 1838, when a young lad out walking on the moors came across the body. Hearing the faint cries for help, the boy scurried down a small embankment and came upon the mortally wounded traveller.

From the powder burns to the face it appeared that whoever had shot the man had done so from a very close range and as help was being summoned, Henderson managed to weekly gasp: "I have been robbed" before slipping unconscious. He died two hours later.

It was learned that Henderson had arranged to meet a fellow traveller, Benjamin Birrell at the 'Five Houses' beer-house on the route through. Birrell told police that he had reached the rendezvous point at 10am and had waited for an hour but with a pressing appointment he was forced to venture on alone, leaving word at the inn that Henderson should now meet up with him in Belmont.

It was common practice for travellers to ride in pairs whenever possible, which apart from the company also lessened the chances of being robbed.

By a terrible misfortune, Henderson was delayed through fog and arriving a little after noon he found his friend had gone on ahead and after a short rest he set out on the fog covered moor alone.

Henderson travelled the first part of the journey a few yards behind a young lad, Thomas Whowell, who was taking lunch to his elder brother at a nearby pit. The two spoke as Whowell stopped and Henderson passed. After completing his errand, Whowell set off again, following the trail taken by the Scotsman. He had only travelled a hundred yards when, despite the thick fog, he saw a patch of blood on the path. As he stopped, he heard faint whimpering coming from a nearby ditch. Taking a closer look, he found himself looking down on the battered and bleeding traveller.

By the time an inquest was held on Henderson at the Blundell Arms, Chorley Old Road, four days later, police already had a man in custody. Twenty-two year old collier James Whittle occupied a cottage at Winter Hill, close to where the body was found. Whittle was the second man to be held for the murder; the first, a poacher seen carrying a gun on the moors, was able to clear his name and was soon released.

Reporters from across the country packed the Blundell Arms, as evidence was heard from Birrell about a man seen on the moors shortly before the murder. Dressed in a long blue coat and carrying a gun, the man asked Birrell if he had seen two men pass by. Birrell replied that he hadn't and carried on ahead. For some reason a sixth sense caused him to turn around, and as he did so he saw the man raise his gun and take aim.

As Birrell spun round the man calmly lowered the gun and asked if had seen that bird fly past, and then offered to show him a short cut across the moors. Wisely, Birrell refused his offer and made off quickly.

Other evidence was heard, most notably from Joseph Halliwell who claimed to have heard a gunshot followed by a man in a blue coat running past him down the path. Asked if he would recognise the man in the blue coat, Halliwell pointed at Whittle who was between two constables and declared: "That's the man I saw!".

Other witnesses testified that Whittle had been in possession of a hunting gun which he had been seen shooting earlier on the morning of September 9th.

The inquest ended with a verdict of murder against Whittle and he was committed for trial at the next Liverpool Assizes in April 1839. Whittle's defence worked hard in casting doubt on

MURDER
AND ROBBERY.
100 POUNDS REWARD

WHEREAS,

A Cruel and Atrocious Murder and Robbery was committed on the person of GEORGE HENDERSON, a Traveller between Five Houses and Belmont, on FRIDAY last, the 9th Instant, who was Shot at with a GUN.

This is to give Notice,

That a REWARD of One Hundred Pounds, will be given to any Person or Persons, who, after this date, shall give such information as may lead to the detection and conviction of the Murderer or Murderers, by applying to

MR. WILLIAM JARDINE,
JOHN STREET, BLACKBURN.

Blackburn, November 11th, 1838.

J. BURRELL, PRINTER, GAZETTE-OFFICE, CHURCH STREET, BLACKBURN.

Henderson's employers had this poster made offering a reward for information leading to the arrest of his killer. It was never claimed.

the evidence the prosecution witnesses had given, but the crux came when they asked Birrell if he could identify the man in the blue coat as the prisoner in the dock. In all honesty, Birrell replied that although he strongly resembled him he couldn't swear on oath. Whittle's counsel pointed out that if Birrell had failed to positively identify him and he had spoken to the man in the blue coat, then in all likelihood Halliwell was mistaken in his identification, bearing in mind that he had merely seen him rushing past.

Halliwell made a poor showing in court, frequently contradicting himself and to further cast doubt on the jury's mind, Whittle's counsel asked if the shooting could be the result of an accident, and asked them to consider if maybe: "Henderson had strayed into the path of a poachers bullet?".

The prosecution contested the last point by saying that the powder burns on the man's face suggested the gun had been fired at close range, effectively ruling out the chance of a stray bullet, but doubt was cast amongst members of the jury, for when they returned a verdict after deliberating for a little over an hour it was in favour of the prisoner. "We find the prisoner James Whittle not guilty of murder", the foreman informed the Judge.

The man in the blue coat was never identified and no-one else was ever charged with the murder.

POSTSCRIPT: So who did kill the traveller on the moors? Looking back at evidence, it appeared that James Whittle was very lucky to

In Memory Of
George Henderson
Traveller
Native of Annan
Dumfrieshire
Who was Barbarously
Murdered on Rivington
Moor
At Noon Day
November 9th 1838
in the 20th year of his age

be acquitted of the charge as many men had gone to gallows on similar testimonies.

Local rumour favoured Whittle as the guilty party. He was well known as a good shot and regularly competed in competitions, often winning good money for those who had backed him. After his ordeal, his aim deteriorated and at his next competition, his backers lost heavily. One was heard to say later that if Whittle's aim had been as good in the competition as it was when he shot the young Scotsman, then they (his fellow gamblers) would now be well off.

Whittle never really recovered from the stigma of the trial, or the suspicions of his neighbours. He was never in good health and lost his sight in middle age, and finally dying in squalor in April 1871.

An iron stump stands on Winter Hill to commemorate the murder of George Henderson by person or persons unknown. An oak stump was placed there in his memory shortly after the murder. The present cast-iron stump has been in place since 1912.

It is called Scotchman's Stump — not because of the victim's nationality but because travellers in the early 19th century were commonly referred to as Scotchmen.

CHAPTER 9

Murder on the Farm

IT was in around 1820 that the future Betty Pilkington met her husband-to-be Robert, a farmer from the Halliwell area of Bolton. Robert Pilkington was aware that Betty had wealthy parents and that they had promised her a dowry, which may have been why he courted and quickly married her. They took over a farm at Pool's Fold, Halliwell, which they ran successfully, and the income was supplemented by rent she received from four cottages left in her legacy; three at Delf Hill and one in the town centre.

They had two sons early in the marriage and Pilkington soon got her to convey the rent from the houses to him, money which he spent on drink. His dissipated habits however, caused them to live unhappily together and in 1835 he attacked her so savagely that he almost killed her.

He was apprehended by the town constable, Mr Robert Makant after a violent struggle which left the officer injured. Fortunately the officer declined against bringing a prosecution, as did his wife, after getting him to sign a separation order and a forfeit of the rent from the cottages, which was put in a trust granting Mrs Pilkington an annual income. Reluctantly Pilkington signed the deed. Betty Pilkington went to live with her sister after the separation until 1837 when she moved in with her eldest son John, who worked a farm at Brownlow Fold. Pilkington junior worked hard building up the farm and three years later he was able to move to a bigger farm, at Langshaw Ford.

Relations between John Pilkington and his father weren't good, and the father was prohibited from entering the farmhouse lest he should cause trouble with his estranged wife and younger son William. Robert Pilkington was allowed to sometimes shelter in the barns on the farm although he spent much of his time lodging with a Mrs Cooper nearby.

Family life was settled until an incident in the Doffcoker public house on March 15th, 1847, when John Pilkington was arrested on a charge of wounding one William Kershaw of Belmont, after a quarrel in the bar. Pilkington was arraigned on

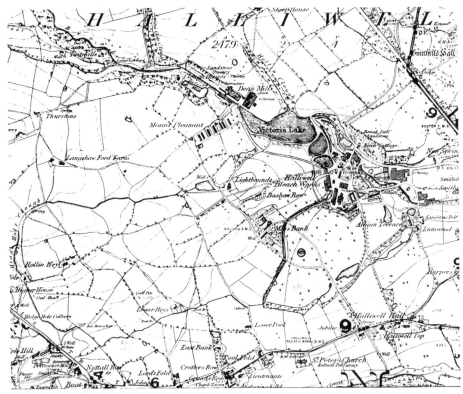

Map of Halliwell showing Langshaw Ford farm.

48

the charge at Liverpool Assizes on August 14th, and five days later sentenced to nine months hard labour at Kirkdale prison.

Word of his son's arrest reached Robert Pilkington and he called at the house extorting money from his wife. When he heard that John had been sent to prison he returned to the farm and announced that he was taking over the running of it in his son's absence.

He was sent away but early on Sunday morning, August 22nd, he returned and asked if he could have a light for his pipe. William said he could do so, provided he left the premises straight away. Pilkington lit his pipe and left only to return again soon after and repeat his intentions of taking over the farm.

Bridget Dean, the young milk-maid at the farm, saw Pilkington on the land, and fearful for the safety of Betty Pilkington, she advised her to accompany her and William in delivering the milk as it would be safer than staying on the farm alone.

The milk delivery took them to the row of houses at nearby Barrow Bridge and after completing their rounds they returned to the farm. At 9am, while William attended to a sick animal in the field, Betty and Bridget entered the farmhouse and found Pilkington sat in the kitchen. They began to quarrel.

"Are you going to be mistress here?", Pilkington asked his estranged wife.

"Yes, our John says I must. And you had better be on your way" she told him.

Pilkington seethed in anger and reaching into the open fire he picked up a large poker and smashed it across her skull killing her instantly. Bridget jumped to Betty's assistance but was knocked to the ground by another blow from the poker, although fortunately for her her injuries were only superficial. Bridget's screams attracted the attention of William and a neighbouring farm hand and they rushed towards the house. Pilkington by this time had made his escape through the back door and had gone before they reached the kitchen.

The local police were summoned along with Dr George

Wolstenholme, who confirmed that Mrs Pilkington had died from a fractured skull caused by the blood stained poker lying in the grate.

The hunt for the killer was a short one. Police Constable Charles Hodgkinson, on duty on Smithhills Dean Road, was warned to be on the look out for Pilkington and shortly before noon he arrested him in that area. Pilkington was heavily bloodstained but denied the murder. When charged back at the station, he replied "Saying so doesn't make it so!"

On Monday morning, Pilkington was brought before the County Sessions Court at Bolton Town Hall, Little Bolton, charged with the murder of his wife, and causing grievous bodily harm to Bridget Dean. After a lengthy hearing, the proceedings ended with him being remanded to appear at Liverpool Assizes in December.

On Thursday, December 16th, 1847, Robert Pilkington was tried before Mr Baron Alderstone. He pleaded not guilty. The prosecution's case was simply that Pilkington had killed his wife in a rage after she had told him he wasn't to be allowed to run his son's farm while the latter was indisposed. Evidence was also heard that he had made repeated threats to his wife and several witnesses testified to hearing him boast that he would kill her if she didn't allow him onto the farm.

His defence counsel, Mr Joseph Pollock, suggested that the prisoner was insane at the time of the attack as a result of a number of previous head wounds. In 1830, he told the court, Pilkington was severely injured when he was run over by a cart. Two years later he received another blow to the head when he was caught up in a disturbance in a public house.

A customer was ejected from the premises for fighting and responded by hurling an empty barrel through the pub window injuring several customers, including the prisoner, who was struck on the head by the barrel. In 1841, he received another blow to the head when he was thrown from a horse.

Mr Pollock also asked the court just to find Pilkington guilty of manslaughter, on account of the hardship he was living under at the time of the attack. Pilkington was homeless whilst his wife had two homes and a large income from other property. The jury were asked to consider the anger he must have felt at his circumstances, which were enough to drive any man to commit a crime.

It was a spirited defence but not enough to convince the jury who returned a verdict of wilful murder. The judge then sentenced the prisoner to be hanged by the neck until dead.

Despite the ferocity of the attack, there was much sympathy for the plight of Pilkington and several appeals were made for a reprieve. His two sons both campaigned for his life, as did the wounded milk-maid and many neighbouring farmers.

Their campaign was rewarded when a telegram was received from London:

"Whitehall January 4th 1848.

Sir. The Home Secretary Sir George Grey, has carefully considered your appeal in behalf of Robert Pilkington, and I have the satisfaction to acquaint you that under all the circumstances of the case, he has felt warranted in advising Her Majesty to commute the sentence to transportation for life. I am, Sir, your most obedient humble servant. J. M. Phillips.

CHAPTER 10

The Great Lever Child Murder

THE tragic discovery that shocked residents of the Great Lever district in the December of 1868 is one of the saddest stories to occupy a place in the annals of Bolton's dark past.

Twenty four year old Sarah Crawford was a single mother with a twelve month old daughter Mary Agnes when she moved from her native Northallerton and settled in Bolton, after first spending a few weeks at Darwen, in the summer of 1868. Whilst in Darwen she had lodged with a kindly old lady and when Sarah enquired about finding work, she was told that there was work going in a Bolton cotton mill. The old lady arranged for Sarah to lodge with her daughter Ellen Kay who lived with her husband in the Rose Hill area of Bolton.

On December 5th, leaving the child in capable hands in Darwen, Sarah arrived at Ellen Kay's door. The Kays already had nine children but managed to find room for Sarah.

The domestic arrangement worked fine until Christmas Eve when Ellen's mother called at the house carrying Sarah's child wrapped in a blanket. She informed Sarah that she could no longer look after Mary and returned her to her mother.

On December 27th, Sarah went out leaving the child to be cared for by Mrs Kay but this arrangement certainly wasn't to her liking. When Sarah returned home that night, Ellen informed her that as she had a number of her own children to look after during the day, she didn't want to, and couldn't even if she had a mind to, look after another, and asked the tearful girl to find alternative accommodation at once.

Later that evening Sarah left the house and returned a short time later telling Ellen that she had arranged to stay with a Mrs Salisbury on Montcrieffe street. At 7-30pm Sarah dressed her daughter in a brown frock and petticoats and left the house.

Two hours later, Sarah returned to the house and told Ellen that she had been unable to get a room with Mrs Salisbury but she had found one on Bridgeman Street. Mrs Kay gave Sarah two shillings and a piece of currant loaf and they parted. She watched Sarah Crawford walk down the street and disappear from the area, not setting eyes on her again until she saw her in the dock at Manchester Assizes.

On the morning of January 2nd, 1869, Thomas Wolstencroft was summoned by his young daughter who claimed that there was a body floating in the lodge adjacent to Ainsworth's mill, Great Lever. He confirmed her discovery and contacted the police.

The identity of the young body was a mystery but when newspaper reports described the clothing that the child had been wearing, they were contacted by Mrs Kay who claimed that they matched those of young Mary who she had last seen a few days before the gruesome discovery. She later positively identified the body as that of Mary Agnes Crawford.

An inquest held before coroner Mr W.S.Rutter at the Bradford Arms found that death was caused by drowning. Police issued an appeal for the mother to come forward. Police staged a huge search for Sarah Crawford who had completely vanished. They learned that she had lost her job just before Christmas and was living on the tiny maintenance money her brother provided for her. Nobody knew the identity of Mary's father as Sarah had never talked about him.

Despite a nationwide search police were unable to locate the woman and gradually the search was scaled down. It was somewhat of a surprise to the duty sergeant at Bolton police station when on February 15th, he looked up from his desk and found Sarah Crawford standing before him.

"I want to give myself up. I killed my little girl. I drowned her in the lodge and there's no use denying it", she told the startled officer.

Sarah was immediately placed under arrest and cautioned. Later that day she made a further statement before being remanded in custody charged with murder.

A few weeks later Sarah Crawford stood trial for her life at the imposing Manchester Assizes. Her defence counsel, Mr Torr, vainly tried to suggest that the death of her child had been the result of an accident and it was really a case of a poor unfortunate, hungry and out of work, frail mother stumbling in the dark and dropping the child into the lodge.

It was a spirited defence, but also a hopeless one. The prosecution pointed to the damning confession made by the prisoner when she surrendered at the police station and pointed out that the likely motive for the murder was the desperate situation that Sarah Crawford had found herself in that Christmas.

Whilst convincing the jury of her guilt, the reference to the poor girl's situation at the time of the murder persuaded them to add a strong recommendation for mercy when they returned a guilty verdict.

Sarah Crawford was duly sentenced to death and removed to the death cell at Strangeways prison. She had no visitors while awaiting execution but just a few short days before she was to die, it was announced that her life had been spared and her sentence was commuted to that of life imprisonment.

CHAPTER 11

Death on Newport Street

WHAT is the cost of a human life? That was the question asked at the conclusion of a tragic case that took place outside Whitfield's beer-house, Newport Street, on a warm late Summer night in 1869.

The events that led to John Heyes ending his life on the steps of the beer-house had began amiably enough. The bar was a popular hang-out for the Irish community in the town and although it had a reputation for trouble, it was usually a safe enough place for workers from the nearby railway yard to visit at the end of their shifts.

On September 6th, John Heyes an Irish labourer in his mid twenties, was sharing a drink at the bar with a group of workmen, one of whom was twenty five year old Henry Horrocks. There had been no trouble during the evening but as Horrocks rose to leave the bar he turned to find Heyes close by his side.

It appeared that Heyes had decided to tag along with Horrocks and his friends who were heading for another local pub for as they reached the door, a witness waiting at a nearby tram-stop heard a man shout: "tha's not comin' with us" and saw Horrocks grab Heyes by the lapels and violently shove him to the ground. Heyes went down with a thud, striking his head on the hard stone flags as he landed.

What happened next was the subject of some conjecture as

various witnesses gave different versions of the events. According to reports in the press, it appeared that Horrocks was then chased from the beer-house by a group of Irishmen. According to one witness, the chase saw Horrocks double back past the doors of Whitfield's beer-house where he was alleged to have kicked out at the stricken man.

Still hotly pursued by a group of Irishmen, Horrocks took refuge in a nearby public house which was a no-go area for the Irishmen. The police were quickly called to Newport street and first aid was given to Heyes, but it was clear he was in a bad way. He was taken home and sent straight to bed. Officers meanwhile had no fear of entering the public house where Horrocks had sought refuge and later that night he was in custody charged with grievous bodily harm.

A week after the attack John Heyes died. The cause of death was put down to inflammation of the brain caused by his head striking the hard flags. The police then charged Horrocks with murder.

When the case reached Manchester Assizes a few weeks later, it had already been decided that Horrocks would only face the lesser charge of manslaughter, but even this carried a very hefty term of imprisonment if he was convicted.

Mr Cottingham led for the prosecution and stated that Horrocks was guilty of a wicked killing which was made even more so by him returning to kick the stricken man as he lay on the ground.

Mr Torr, his defence counsel, disputed the last statement and suggested that while Horrocks was responsible for the death of John Heyes, it was more the result of an unfortunate accident and at no time was there any malice intended. Torr had done his work well for while the jury returned a guilty verdict, as it was the only one possible on the evidence heard before the court, the judge merely sentenced Horrocks to be bound over to the court for the sum of twenty pounds.

Twenty pounds — the small cost of a man's life.

CHAPTER 12

The Trade Union Outrage

THE strike at Slater's bleachworks, Back o'th Bank, in January 1876, started innocuously enough. An order was received for one hundred yards of cloth which was to be bleached and stamped in the corner. The last part of the job, stamping the cloth in the corner as opposed to the usual task of stamping in the middle, involved more work, and therefore took a little longer. As a result, those on piece-work asked for a higher rate of pay.

The manager, Mr Crossley, made them an offer which they rejected, adding that if their demands weren't met they would go on strike. Crossley told them he had no authority to offer more money and suggested that they took up their grievances with the owner Mr Slater. Slater was the archetypal Victorian factory owner. Very strict, he ruled his work-force with a rod of iron and was much feared by his employees.

Slater told the workers elected spokesman that he had no plans to heed to their request as in his view their demands for a pay increase were most unreasonable.

The deadline for the order was fast approaching and in order to dispatch it on time, the under-managers worked through the night to complete the work. Next day was pay-day and those workers who had refused to stamp the cloth in the corners were issued with a dismissal notice. A week later others in the same association (forty-one men and seventeen girls) who had refused to work until there fellow members were re-instated, were also issued with redundancy notices. As a result, workers gathered outside the main gates and formed a picket line.

Although this severely depleted the work-force, those dismissed did not account for the whole complement of workers as many had left the trade union unhappy with its militant leanings.

Slater knew he had little chance in recruiting local men to cross the picket line and therefore advertised for replacement workers in Scottish and Irish newspapers offering on-site accommodation to those who would travel to Bolton to fulfil urgent vacancies. These out of town workers who came mainly from Glasgow and Dublin were christened 'Knob-sticks' by the striking workers, who themselves were known as 'turn-outs'.

Although there was much hostility to these workers and the police were in daily attendance to prevent any trouble, the picketing was relatively peaceful, helped no doubt by the fact that most workers never set foot outside the gates. Trouble, when it did come, was severe and merciless.

At 10-30pm, Saturday, April 8th, three men left the bleach-works and called into the Robin Hood public house for a drink. They were James M'Curley, John Wright and forty year old father of three James Thompson. The first two were 'Knobsticks' who worked as beetlers at the works, the last man was a local man who tended the boiler at the factory. Although Thompson had joined the work-force after the strike had begun, he wasn't a 'knobstick' merely a new worker who would have taken up the position regardless of the industrial action.

All three bought a pint of beer and settled down with their drinks. Their departure from the works had been spotted by a 'turn-out' who followed them into the bar. The 'turn-out' returned to the strike and informed them that there were three 'knobsticks' drinking in the pub.

Finishing their drinks, the three returned to the bleachworks. Thompson was still on duty and had to tend to the boiler, the others were returning to their cottage for a night's sleep. As they walked down Slater's lane towards the factory, they passed under the railway arches of the recently constructed Astley Bridge branch line, where they were ambushed by a gang of men.

One of the 'turn-outs' threw a stone at the men which acted as the signal for other to follow. What happened next was never made clear.

As the 'turn-outs' shouted at the three, Wright turned on his heels and fled. The strikers rushed at the other two and began kicking and punching them. M'Curley was felled by a blow to the face and curled up in a ball on the ground as several men began to kick him with heavy clogs. He escaped with his life and managed to hobble back to the factory.

Thompson had been due to fire the boiler at mid-night before heading for home. He was usually home by 12-30am and when he failed to return his wife asked a neighbour to accompany her to the factory. She had feared for her husband's safety at work in face of the growing tension which in recent weeks had grown noticeably.

Together with Sam Pilkington, her neighbour, and Martha Heapey, her sister, they walked up Slater's lane towards the factory gates. Passing the railway arches they saw what they thought was drunk lying on a piece of wasteland. Pilkington suggested that they turn him over to prevent him choking and as they did so they were horrified to find that the 'drunk' was in fact the bloody and battered body of James Thompson.

The police were summoned at once and acted with such alacrity that by morning they had thirty-four men in custody. All had been identified as having taken an active part in strik-

Thomas Beech, Bolton's Chief Constable at the time of the strike, 1876.

ing outside the bleach-works. The testimonies of both Wright and the injured M'Curley made it clear that the number of attackers were nowhere near thirty-four and after a series of interviews, police released twenty-nine of the men, detaining just five.

On Monday, April 17th, Bolton Borough Court was packed to capacity as a hearing took place to decide what those arrested should be charged with. At 11-30am, Mr Beech, the Chief Constable, went into the dock and called out the names of the accused. They were:

Edwin Ashcroft (30), a crofter, of Devonshire St.

James Atkin (25), of Deansgate.

John Barnes (25), of Hill street.

Thomas Ainsworth (25), of Moss street.

Thomas Haslam (36), of Bury Old Road.

Atkins was defended by Mr Richardson, the rest were defended by Mr Fielding, who had caused an uproar at an earlier hearing when he claimed he had been unable to speak to his clients after their arrest, which he claimed was illegal.

Mr John Hall prosecuted and as the hearing went into a second day, another prisoner was put up in the dock. Twenty-six year old Edward Birch was arrested at the house he lodged at on Cable street. The hearing ended when all six were arraigned to stand trial at Manchester in the summer.

The trial of the Bolton 'turn-outs' took place before Mr Baron Bramwell on July 14th, at Manchester Crown Court. The men were charged:

*'that on April 8th, 1876, they feloniously, wilfully and
with malice aforethought, killed and murdered one James
Thompson.'*

Mr Higgin QC, the prosecutor told the court of the events
that led to the tragedy. He alleged that it was Atkins who had
followed the three workers into the public house, and that all
six were pickets told to watch out for 'knobsticks' and to chal-
lenge them if they saw them out drinking.

Higgin claimed that since the remand hearing three of the
men, Haslam, Barnes and Ashworth had turned Queen's evidence and testified against the others.

The jury retired after hearing all the evidence and returned
to find the three guilty of manslaughter. In his summing up, it
was clear who the Judge felt was the more guilty of the three.
He pointed out that both Ainsworth and Atkins were former
workers who had been made redundant over a matter of prin-
ciple, while Birch had no connection with the dispute and had
assumed the role of a 'flying picket'. He then passed sentences
of fifteen years on Birch, ten years on Ainsworth, and seven
years on Atkins. The three who had turned Queens Evidence,
were arraigned on a Coroner's warrant and released.

The case made headlines across the country and was reported in one London paper thus:

*James Thompson was stoned and kicked to death at
Bolton because his views of political economy and his conduct as influenced by these views did not coincide with the
views of the three convicted men.*

*There is little doubt that they didn't mean to kill Thom-
pson, merely that they had expected a fight, having at one
stage tried to engage the services of a local tough, for the
sum of thirty pence, to beat up the workers.*

The report ended with the following comment:

*"Will it ever be recognised that clogs are at least a
deadly weapon as knives and the revolver".*

CHAPTER 13

The St. Patrick's Night Murder

W HEN eighteen year old William Cooper spotted Ellen Smith across the floor in a Bolton dance hall, in the summer of 1855, his heart skipped a beat and he hurried over to renew their acquaintance. He remembered Ellen at once from his younger days — they had grown up in the same Daubhill streets — and overcoming his shyness, he asked her to dance. She agreed to his request and they walked onto the dance floor together. They spent much of the summer together and their friends and family thought them ideally suited, but dark clouds soon loomed on the horizon.

One evening Cooper turned up for a meeting and found her talking to another man, a friend of her brother's. He waited until the man walked away, then confronted her. She angrily told him not to be so jealous and that he was getting worked up for nothing, but the seeds of suspicion had been sowed.

Two days later they had another quarrel and she told him they were finished. A week without her new love was enough and she made plans to see him again, only to be horrified to learn that not only had he left home, but he had given up his job and enlisted in the East India Regiment, being posted overseas. Reluctantly she put him to the back of her mind and getting on with life, she soon met another man.

In the spring of 1859, Cooper left the army and returned to Bolton. The long years away had caused him to forget the reason for his break up with Ellen, and he was looking forward to seeing her again, hopeful for a quick reconciliation.

Unfortunately for Cooper, in the cruelest twist of fate, the very day his ship landed in port, Ellen had walked down the aisle with James Mather, and when he arrived home she was away on her honeymoon.

It was several months before he saw her again. They met by chance in a dance hall and began to discuss what each had been up to since that fateful row two years earlier. They parted on pleasant terms and got on with their own lives.

In 1872 James Mather decided to seek his fortune in America and the couple split up. Mather took three of their four sons with him, leaving Ellen to look after the youngest, aged nine.

The Albert, Derby Street.

To make ends meet she went back to work as a barmaid at the Albert, a public house on Derby Street, Bolton, leaving the child in the care of her mother.

It was possibly again by chance that Cooper, now forty years old, married with a young family, and working as a foreman brass moulder, walked into the bar one evening and spotted her. He learned of her separation and from then on he became a frequent visitor to the pub, even though it was a fair distance from his Kearsley home. He soon made clear his intentions of starting up the relationship again but any romantic feelings she had for him had long since gone, and she told him so, but she had a fondness for her old flame and would often drink with him.

On St Patrick's night, 1879, the landlady of the Albert, Mrs Leach, asked Ellen and another barmaid, Mrs Waring, the landlady's sister, if they would like to earn some extra money by waiting on at a dance she was catering for at the Bridgeman Street Assembly Hall, close to Bolton town centre. The pair agreed, and at closing time they set off down Derby street towards the town.

When Cooper heard where she was going he became angry. He cast his mind back only to last Christmas when she had last helped out at the hall. He remembered her flirting with more than one customer and when he asked her to walk home with him she had shrugged him off and he became mad with jealousy as she walked home with another.

He asked her not to work at the hall but she told him it was none of his business and besides, she needed the extra money. He pleaded with her not to go but she told him to go home and carried on walking. Cooper walked slowly behind.

The two women reached Trinity Street station, where he again pleaded with her not to go to the dance. When she again ignored his request he slapped her across the face. "You don't go there tonight", he told her. She cursed him. "What is it with you?, why don't you just go home and mind your own wife and leave me be?"

The words hit home hard and in an instant he grabbed her by the neck, put his knee into her back and forcing her head down, he quickly withdrew a pocket knife and cut her throat.

Mrs Waring began shrieking: "Murder!, Murder", and within minutes a policeman arrived on the scene, to whom Cooper

Trinity Church, Trinity Street.

calmly handed the knife. "You've no need to get hold of me", he told the officer, "I'm not going to run, I've done what I intended".

Cooper stood over the mortally wounded woman lying in a pool of blood and mumbled: "Bless thee, bless th' corpse if thou'rt dead!". He then bent down to kiss her but was held back. Looking up at the constable, Ellen managed to whisper "He's a bad un. I hope he will suffer", before she slipped into unconsciousness. She was taken to the home of Dr Johnstone on Deansgate, but Ellen was beyond help and she passed away a few hours later by which time Cooper was already in custody. He was then charged with wilful murder.

On Monday, April 28th, 1879, he stood trial at Manchester Assizes. His defence was that he was not guilty of murder, but guilty of manslaughter committed 'in a frenzy of passion'. His counsel also argued that Cooper had no knowledge of what he was doing at the time of the attack but it was a forlorn hope and the jury took just seven minutes to find him guilty.

On Tuesday, May 28th, William Cooper was hanged at Strangeways prison by the country's chief executioner, William Marwood.

CHAPTER 14

Mercy for William Bradburn

A T Manchester Assizes on July 14th, 1882, Mr Justice Day sentenced thirty-two year old Farnworth collier William Bradburn to be 'hanged by the neck until you are dead'. His crime had been brutal enough but many in the packed courtroom thought the sentence was harsh and it would be a grave miscarriage of justice if the hangman was allowed to place his rope around Bradburn's neck.

The chain of events leading to Bradburn, a widower, standing to forfeit his life, began on a damp Wednesday morning ten weeks earlier when neighbours in the Longcauseway district of Farnworth were horrified to see a semi-naked man rush from his house in Kay street and stagger down the road bleeding from a hideous gash in his throat. Several watched as the man faltered a hundred yards down the road and then collapsed in a heap.

Neighbours rushed to his assistance and as a number carried him home, one called for Dr Clarke whose surgery was just around the corner. The doctor hurried to attend to Bradburn and immediately began to stitch the gaping wound in his neck. Agnes Farnworth his close neighbour offered to make him up a bed in her sitting room but as she had no clean blankets she went upstairs to see if Bradburn had any in his airing cupboard.

Mrs Farnworth climbed the staircase and entering the front bedroom she recoiled in horror at the sight before her. Lying in their beds were the bodies of his two children, step-daughter Pheobe Hardy (17), and his own son Peter aged nine. Both had wounds to the throat; the boy's windpipe had been completely severed. Pheobe's throat had been slit halfway across, but both had had their deaths hastened by a severe battering about the head. Dr Clarke examined them and concluded they had been dead for several hours.

The police were summoned and although Bradburn was unable make a statement he wrote down the address of his mother in Irlam and she was contacted and brought to his bedside. Detectives were at a loss as to the motive for the brutal killings and although his mother told them that Bradburn had a history of mental illness, he had been living a normal family life for many years, during which time he had come through the bereavement of losing his wife without breaking down, and it seemed that something must have acted as a catalyst.

It was whilst searching through some personal papers in Bradburn's room that a likely motive came to light. A letter dated April 30th was found written by Bradburn to his mother, but never posted, which revealed that a relationship between his step-daughter and the son of a local inn-keeper was driving him crazy.

Pheobe, it seems had confided in him that she had been secretly seeing the young man, one Thomas Houghton, for some time, but she had only admitted to it when Houghton had begun to abuse and ill-treat her. The letter described how Bradburn had sent two young girls around to Houghton's house asking him to call at the Bradburn's Kay Street home on Tuesday night.

Houghton had agreed to make the visit but later changed his mind and went to drill practice with his local army volunteer unit.

Police interviewed Houghton and he confirmed that parts of the letter were true but he denied ill-treating Pheobe. Detectives told the young lad that by breaking the appointment he had in all probability saved his own life.

What they didn't tell him though, is that it was possible that his failure to show up had sent Bradburn into a mad rage during which he had turned on his own children.

The whole sorry tale came out when the case appeared before Mr Justice Day at the Assizes a few months later and despite a spirited defence at the trial, during which evidence was shown that Bradburn had spent several periods of his life at Prestwich mental asylum, the jury returned to find Bradburn guilty of wilful murder and the trial ended with the passing of the death sentence.

JUSTICE DAY.

The people of Farnworth with full backing of the local press urged the Home Secretary to reprieve Bradburn who was scheduled to be hanged at Strangeways on August 7th. As the date of the execution approached there was still no word of a reprieve, indeed, the only mention of Bradburn's fate was the chilling sentence that hangman Marwood had accepted the engagement to carry out the sentence. Finally, the news that most people in the area wanted to here came in the form of an official telegram addressed to the leader of the campaign, Rev D S Prosser of Walkden:

> *"Whitehall July 27th, 1882 - Sir - with reference to your application on behalf of William Bradburn, I am directed by the Secretary of State to acquaint you that he has been pleased, having regard to all the circumstances of the case, to advise her Majesty to commute the sentence of death passed upon this man, to one of penal servitude for life.*
>
> *A. F. O. Liddell*

CHAPTER 15

Shots at the Big House

CAPTAIN Thomas Chester Andsell's imposing residence on Kearsley Moss was known among the locals as "The Big House". The wealthy Captain, who had long since retired from a long exciting career in the militia, employed a number of servants to help him through his twilight years, and numbered amongst these were Abraham Thomas and Mrs Christiana Leigh.

Twenty-four year old Thomas held the position of butler, while Mrs Leigh some fifteen years older, acted as house-keeper, and the complement of staff was filled with a coach-man, a gardener and two maids.

Mrs Leigh was the senior member of the 'downstairs staff' and as such was placed in charge of running the house when-ever the Captain was away. This wasn't the normal practice in large houses, where the butler wasn't under the control of the housekeeper, and this, it seemed, caused Thomas to resent the authority of Mrs Leigh.

On December 22nd, 1882, Captain Andsell left the house to spend the festivities with his daughter, telling his staff he would be back in the new year.

The departure by the Captain seemed to be a cue for Thomas to ease off his duties and start celebrating his Christmas a few days early. On the following morning he was given a warning for being late on duty and later that afternoon he was again cautioned, this time for being drunk. Relations between Thomas and the housekeeper were very strained and it was soon clear that he was due for a reprimand when his boss returned.

True to her word, the day Captain Andsell returned, Mrs Leigh visited him in his study and informed him of the butler's unsatisfactory conduct. Thomas was given a message that until the Captain could have chance to interview him at length, he was being suspended from duty and told to hand his keys in.

On the following morning, January 4th, 1883, Thomas reported for duty at the house but was reminded he was under suspension and told to go home. Instead of leaving he went into the gardens where he was seen by the gardener entering the photographic studio. The studio also housed the Captain's hunting guns.

When Mrs Leigh came on duty she was told that Thomas was on the premises and set out at once to find him. She entered the studio and moments later a shot rang out. A housemaid ran to investigate and was confronted with the sight of Thomas standing over the body of the housekeeper with a smoking gun in his hand.

The police were called at once and Thomas offered no resistance as he was taken into custody. Asked what had happened, he could only reply "I don't know. We didn't get on very well, but I didn't know what I was doing".

Three weeks later Thomas found himself before Mr Justice Key at Manchester Assizes. There was no doubt that the sad, dejected looking figure in the dock was the man who had pulled the trigger, but was he guilty of a cold wicked, calculated murder, as the prosecution claimed, or was he insane as the defence maintained?

His counsel claimed that Thomas suffered from a rare brain disorder 'brain fever' they called it, and as such whenever he had a drink he would become insane. Unfortunately for the prisoner, the 19th Century doctors hadn't yet began to fully understood mental illness and as a result it didn't carry much weight in court.

More damning was the fact that a loaded shot-gun was found in Thomas's quarters at the house. The gun was the matching pair to the murder weapon, which he had been cleaning prior to the murder. The fact that it was in his room and loaded, against the house rules, suggested that he had an ulterior motive in stashing it away. Had he pre-planned the shooting, and was this the gun he had intended to commit the murder with?

Listening to both sides of the case the jury sided with the prosecution and the Judge was left to pass the only sentence the law prescribed for murder.

On February 12th, 1883, Abraham Thomas was hanged at Strangeways prison. He told a friend on the day before he was hanged that he was very sorry and expressed great penitence over what he had done.

Strangeways Prison, where Abraham Thomas paid for his crime.

CHAPTER 16

The Astley Bridge Wife Murder

THERE was a large crowd gathering in Astley Bridge as word spread that there had been an 'orrible murder on Coop Street. At eight o'clock that Tuesday morning, January 26th, 1883, Hugh Calderbank, a fifty-three year old, unemployed cotton worker, had called on his next door neighbour and asked if their young son would run an errand for him. The young lad was told to call at a nearby cotton mill and tell Calderbank's twenty-three year old daughter Margaret to return home at once.

Within a short time Margaret arrived at the house and found her father sitting in the kitchen with a dazed look on his face. "What is it, dad?" she asked, as he began to sob. He told her to go into the bedroom, but scared of what she might find, Margaret went next door and asked her neighbour to accompany her.

They quickly returned and entering the darkened room, she made out the shape of her mother lying on the bed. "She's dead!", Calderbank cried, having followed them into the room. The neighbour quickly left and hurried to nearby Astley Bridge police station and summoned Sergeant Jack Sullivan.

"I've strangled her", Calderbank said, turning to his daughter before picking up his coat and walking outside. Margaret set off in pursuit.

When the police officer returned with the neighbour they examined the body and thought at first that she had died of natural causes and it was only when Margaret returned with her father that they learned of his confession. Calderbank was then placed under arrest and taken into custody.

An inquest was held in which evidence was given describing the relationship between the victim and her husband. Isabella Calderbank was forty-seven years old at the time of her death. She was his second wife and they had been married fourteen years, although during the last few years the marriage was under a considerable strain. This was partly because they were both out of work and preferred to spend the days drinking in the local pub, and the nights at home fighting and arguing.

Although Calderbank was a large, healthy and strong man, he was often rebuked by his wife who seemed to make a habit of putting him down, usually after drink and nearly always when she had an audience. Many of their friends wondered if, or more likely when, the inoffensive respectable family man would finally turn on his wife.

Calderbank's nineteen year old son told the inquest that on the night before the murder his parents had been on good

HORRIBLE WIFE MURDER NEAR BOLTON.

Another terrible tragedy has occured in the Bolton district, the locality this time being Astley Bridge, a mile and a half beyond Bolton on the way to Blackburn. An operative cotton spinner named Hugh Calderbank had been quarrelling with his wife through her intemperate habits. This morning she was found lying in bed dead with' black marks on her neck, and the husband acknowledged that he had strangled her.

terms during the evening and neither of them were drunk. They had all retired to bed and at 5-15am next morning, John had risen and gone to work, his parents both blissfully asleep as he crept out in the darkness.

Neighbours rising later that morning testified that they heard raised voices from the Calderbank home, and claimed that this was a continuation of a quarrel from the previous evening, but this didn't tally with what Calderbank's son had stated. It was only after the young neighbour had been sent to summon Margaret from work that it became clear what terrible deed had taken place in the house.

The inquest concluded with Calderbank being remanded to stand trial at Liverpool Assizes later that Spring.

At the subsequent trial, evidence was heard of the sequence of events prior to the tragedy. Doctors testified that Calderbank had strangled his wife by pressing his thumb and fingers against her windpipe.

His defence was to be that he was insane. The family doctor claimed that in the weeks prior to the tragedy, Calderbank had lost a lot of weight and had taken to sporting a strange look on his face. In the week prior to the crime, he had knotted a sheet from the bed and tried to hang himself but had been unable to finish the job before his wife came home.

The doctor was not able to say for sure if the prisoner was capable of judging the rights and wrongs of his actions on the night of the murder, but was prepared to say that in his opinion Calderbank was suffering from 'manic insanity'.

So strong was the case of insanity put, that after this evidence had been given, the Judge, Mr Justice Key, invited the jury to consider if Calderbank was suffering from insanity. They took only a few moments to return a verdict of 'not guilty to wilful murder, on the grounds of insanity'.

Calderbank was sentenced to be detained in prison during 'Her Majesty's pleasure'.

CHAPTER 17

Murder and Suicide on Churchgate

IN the spring of 1883, sixty-four year old Peter Kelly along with his wife Ellen (58) and their daughter Maria, took residence of a small cottage on Antelope Court, opposite the Man and Scythe, on Churchgate. The cottage was on the path to the disused Settle School and was owned by the same people, and part of the tenancy agreement was that the occupants had to tend to the upkeep of the old school for a small wage.

This arrangement initially suited Kelly who chose to retire after a long career with the same Eagley engineering firm. However, as the date for his retirement neared, Kelly became morose and despondent at the impending retirement and received treatment from a doctor. The doctor recorded that he thought Kelly was suffering from depression and needed to be watched.

The retirement went ahead as planned but not long after he began to turn on his wife, frequently slapping her and being generally cruel. In early July, after a particularly angry quarrel with his wife, he climbed up to the second floor window and tried to hurl himself out. He was prevented from doing so by his daughter who took a firm grip of his legs and held on grimly until help could arrive.

He was again treated by the doctor who diagnosed a serious mental condition but Kelly refused his offer of a stay in a mental asylum. With strong personal reasons.

On Tuesday, July 17th, Kelly and his wife went to visit their eldest daughter who was an inmate at the Fishpool Asylum. The visit seemed to greatly distress him.

Next day he was visited by his younger brother Patrick who along with his young wife ran a local pub, the Bradford Arms on Foundary street. The two brothers chatted for a while and each drank a glass of hot whiskey. They were joined by Ellen Kelly who also took a drink. Patrick asked Ellen how she had received the black eye that was fading but still visible, and she told him that Pete had done it during a quarrel.

Peter Kelly rose from his chair and went outside, returning minutes later with an axe which he swung over his head. His wife and brother tensed up and watched in horror but relaxed when he lowered the axe and left the room. They exchanged glances and breathed a sigh of relief.

Almost at once, Peter Kelly ran back into the room this time swing the axe wildly. He struck his brother a heavy blow to the shoulder, sending him reeling, before knocking his wife against the fender where she slumped unconscious. With a wild glare on his face Peter Kelly lashed out repeatedly at his brother who was unable to fend off the blows and became a mass of blood and bruises as the relentless attack continued for almost a minute.

Eventually Peter Kelly threw the axe to the ground and ran upstairs, heading for the second floor bedroom window, where a week earlier he had been prevented from hurling himself through. This time there was no-one to stop him and crashing through the glass he dived two floors down onto the stone fore-court.

Remarkably both Kelly brothers were alive when taken into

hospital, but Peter Kelly died soon after admittance. Patrick was able to tell police what had happened before he slipped into unconsciousness. He died in the following week from his terrible injuries. Mrs Kelly made a full recovery.

POSTSCRIPT: The new tax office now occupies the site close to what was once Antelope Court. For many years the ABC cinema stood on the very same spot where this terrible crime was committed. Workers at the cinema claimed to have seen the figure of an old man prowling the premises. Was Peter Kelly that gruesome spectre?

New Tax Office,
Churchgate.

CHAPTER 18

A Just Reward

THERE is a saying that you get what you deserve, and there are few more deserving of that saying than forty year old Farnworth collier John Royle.

John Royle's second marriage had ended acrimoniously. The burly collier had fallen out with his wife who ran the Bull's Head Inn, Market street, Farnworth and one spring night, in 1884, he had walked out on her. Not content with stealing their joint savings of over fifty pounds, he stole away after first turning on all the beer taps and flooding the cellar.

Royle had often spoken of emigrating to America and it was assumed that with him stealing their savings, this had been his aim. He had in fact travelled only as far as Yorkshire where he stayed with a friend for a short time before returning to his fathers house at Manor Cottage, Kearsley, finding work in the local pit.

It didn't take long for the widower and father of three to re-gret his hasty decision to part from his new wife. He wrote her a long letter apologising for his misdeeds and asked to come home. She refused and when he turned up in the bar she had him escorted off the premises. Not only this but on the advice of a friend she took out a court order against her husband, which prevented him from entering the Inn.

He tried one last attempt to persuade her to change her mind but when she returned his letter un-opened he finally realised the marriage was broken beyond repair and decided on drastic action.

It was in the early hours of a still Sunday morning, June 8th, when Royle approached the door of the Inn. He was well versed in the movements of those on the premises, which that weekend comprised of his wife and two female servants, Polly Bromilow and Alice Wild whose quarters were in the front bedroom. There was one other occupant on the premises who Royle didn't know about. After hearing that Royle had been making drunken threats that he would 'do for' his wife, she had taken the precaution of buying a large retriever dog 'Carlo' which slept at the foot of her bed.

Royle prised open the trap door and dropped in to darkened cellar. He removed his heavy clogs and crept silently along the passage up the foot of the stairs, pausing only to pick up the heavy axe that he knew was kept in the kitchen.

Removing a length of rope he had coiled over his shoulder, he tightly knotted one end to the servants bedroom door knob, and the other to the bannister, thereby preventing anybody disturbing him while he went about his terrible mission.

Slipping into his wife's bedroom, Royle pulled out a small chisel from his pocket and strode across to the bed with a weapon in either hand. It was only as he neared the edge of the bed that he realised the presence of the dog. Alerted by the intruder, the dog began to bark, and in an effort to silence it, he lashed out with his foot. The commotion woke his wife and lighting her bedside candle she saw her husband grappling with the dog.

"Is that you, John?", Mary Royle cried. "Whatever are you doing here? she shouted as he moved closer. His chilling reply was: "Yes, it's me. I'll let you see what I've come for - I've come to murder you with this axe, and by God I'll do it".

Royle kicked the dog aside and swung the axe at his wife as she tried to scramble out of the bed. She received a number of wounds from the axe before managing to crawl under the large bed. The dog yelped pitifully before scurrying away in sheer terror.

The sound of the disturbance had woken the servants and after frantic tugging at the door handle they had managed to free themselves and hurry to her assistance. They dashed into the mistresses bedroom where they were confronted by her axe wielding husband, who wasted no time in turning on them. Royle swung the axe with such force that the axe-head flew off and although he managed to strike the servants with the shaft where both received a savage beating before managing to force Royle out of the bedroom.

One of the servants ran downstairs and out into the front street shouting "Help!, Murder!". It was then, as the would-be murderer re-traced his steps towards the cellar, that fate caught up with John Royle. Unable to find his footing in the dimly lit corridor, he stumbled over the top stair and fell crashing down onto the stone cellar floor, where he lay motionless.

Amongst the first people to the scene was the local doctor who after seeing that although both servants were seriously wounded, none of the victims were in any immediate danger, made his way into the cellar. Examining the prone figure, the doctor confirmed that John Royle was dead, and that he had died from a broken neck sustained in the fall.

Lying next to the body was a smashed rum bottle which had slipped out of his pocket as he fell. It bore the label of the Clarence Hotel, Bradshawgate, Bolton, where Royle had been drinking prior to the attack and where he had managed to summon up the courage to commit his crime.

An inquest was later held at the Bowling Green and for a time it seemed that both Mrs Royle and Mrs Bromilow might succumb to their injuries, while Carlo, the retriever, was found cowering in a nearby back alley a few days later.

Royle's son claimed that his father had been out on Saturday night but had returned home to bed sober at 10-45pm. The lad said that his father must have slipped out of the house while he was asleep.

The autopsy had found that Royle was drunk when he at-

THE ATTEMPTED TRIPLE MURDER AT FARNWORTH.

It has now been ascertained positively that the man Royle did not poison himself, but that he broke his neck by falling down the cellar after the attack on his wife and the servants. The women are both expected to recover if erysipelas can be averted. The bottle found near the dead man had contained spirits, which he had apparently drunk to nerve himself for the crime.

tempted to kill his wife. The rum he had drank to gain courage to carry out the dreadful deed, had had the opposite effect.

Instead of Mrs Royle lying on the pathologist's slab, her place was taken by John Royle, who had received his just reward.

POSTSCRIPT: The funeral of John Royle took place a week after his death and was witnessed by thousands of locals who crowded the streets leading to Farnworth Cemetery. He was buried in the next plot to the two Bradburn children (see chapter 14).

CHAPTER 19

The Death of a Salesman

O N Friday morning, October 3rd, 1884, thirty-seven year old Richard Dugdale left his lodging in Bolton town centre and set out on his rounds. Dugdale's home was in Wakefield and his job as a salesman with the Castleford Brewery, meant he was often away for long periods, but today he reasoned that if he made an early start, and with a bit of luck, he would be able to catch the evening train and be home with his wife and young family for the weekend.

His first call was at the Greyhound Inn on Manchester road, where after pocketing a cheque for eight pounds, he returned to the town centre for a meeting with a colleague in the Fleece on Bradshawgate. The appointment was planned for 10-30am, but thirty minutes later the friend still hadn't shown. At 11am, he was joined by Robert Hall, an oil merchant from Eagley who knew Dugdale from his previous job in the licensing trade. The two men were sharing a drink and a chat when they were joined by Kay Howarth, a twenty-five years old, stocky, tough looking man who sported a large moustache.

Hall knew Howarth well enough to know that he wasn't the sort of person he would invite to join their company, for he was well known in town centre pubs as a sponger and loafer. Howarth was also a petty thief.

Forcing himself upon the two, he soon managed to elicit a

drink from Dugdale and when the two decided to go for lunch, Howarth tagged along. He did pay for his own food out of a two shilling piece which he claimed was all the money he had in the world.

The non-showing of his 10-30am appointment meant that Dugdale would have to stay the night in Bolton and chase up the client in the morning, and the men then spent the afternoon drinking in numerous town centre pubs while Dugdale carried out the rest of his business. During one of his transactions Dugdale returned to the table clutching a number of gold sovereigns.

By 6pm, Dugdale was drunk, and Hall, who had a business appointment himself, asked Howarth if he would escort his friend to the Wheatsheaf Inn where he was staying. The men were seen walking down Deansgate at 7pm, with Howarth having to sup-

Richard Dugdale.

Kay Howarth

port his new friend, but when Howarth bumped into Hall again later that night in the Crown and Cushion he was alone.

When asked where Dugdale was Howarth said he had left him in the Balmoral where they had gone for a drink. "We had an argument", Howarth told him, "and I left after he began to call me names for not being able to stand a round".

Hall said he would go to the Balmoral to check on him, but Howarth said he wont be in there as he had followed him out, "I last saw him walking down Mawdesley street", he claimed.

Hall called at the Wheatsheaf hoping that his friend had retired for the night but was told that he wasn't in. Much as he would have liked to satisfy himself that his friend was safe, it was getting late and he had a tram to catch.

At 9pm, Richard Dugdale was found dead. A resident in Silverwell Street was about to dispose of some bottles on a patch of wasteland when he saw what he thought was a drunk lying on the ground. He deliberately smashed one of the bottles, hoping that the sound would frighten the 'drunk' into moving off, but when the man remained motionless he ventured over and took a closer look.

Silverwell Street, where Dugdale's body was found.

The man's face was contorted and he bore a deep gash in his throat. The police were called and from beside the body they removed a note book which revealed his name. From the entries in it it showed that the man had collected a large sum of money on his travels but his pockets were quiet empty.

This contradicted the note the man was clutching in his hand which said "good-bye all". In his other hand was a blood-stained pocket knife. It was clear to the policeman that there had been a clumsy attempt to make it appear that Dugdale had committed suicide. The body was removed to the mortuary at School Hill where a police doctor was soon able to confirm that the man had been murdered.

Detectives re-traced Dugdale's steps during that Friday afternoon and soon learned that he had spent most of the day with Bob Hall. In the early hours police called at Hall's house in Eagley and asked him about his movements that evening. Hall's reaction was one of genuine shock and he told the police that Dugdale had last been in the company of Kay Howarth.

The name was known to police and within the hour they called at his home. Howarth claimed he knew nothing of the murder but sharp eyed detectives spotted blood on his trousers and a search of his room soon unearthed Dugdale's watch and chain. In a jacket pocket police found over thirty-two pounds in gold coins plus the eight pound cheque. Howarth claimed that Dugdale had given him them for safe keeping.

THE BOLTON MURDER.

EXECUTION
OF
KAY HOWARTH.

HIS CLOSING MOMENTS.

SCENE ON THE SCAFFOLD.

This morning, at eight o'clock, Kay Howarth was executed within the precincts of Strangeways Gaol, Manchester, for the wilful murder of Richard Dugdale, at Bolton, on the 3rd of October last. In the case of Howarth no attempt had been made to get up a petition for his reprieve and avert the execution of the capital sentence. Both during his trial and up to within a day or two ago the condemned man had maintained a cool and stolid

To expect police to believe that Howarth and Dugdale had fallen out in the pub, as Howarth had told Hall and repeated to the officers when first questioned, and then to say that Dugdale had given him the items to safeguard against theft was the act of a desperate man and after a caution, Howarth was charged with wilful murder and arrested.

On November 6th, Howarth found himself in the dock at Manchester Assizes before Mr Justice Smith. Evidence was heard that Howarth was short of money before meeting Dugdale, yet after offering to escort him home, he returned to the Crown and Cushion brandishing a bulging wallet. The man's guilt was never in doubt and the court was packed throughout the eleven hours by many Boltonians who filled the gallery.

The jury needed just fifteen minutes to find Howarth guilty and he was condemned to death. He spent the last days of his life in the condemned cell at Strangeways prison in a cool and unafraid manner but on the morning of his execution, as the hangman James Berry led him to the drop he burst into tears as he saw the noose. Moments later Richard Dugdale was avenged.

CHAPTER 20

An Unhappy Household

A SAD case of domestic unhappiness was brought to an abrupt close when the gallows crashed open at Strangeways prison on a warm May morning in 1887. The culprit who paid for his crime was thirty-five year old Bolton mill worker Walter Wood; his crime: the cruel murder of his wife.

Walter Wood met his pretty wife Emma while both were employed in a Bury mill. They found they had a lot in common, but what brought them together was the fact that they had both recently been widowed. After a brief courtship, Walter, a father of two, proposed to Emma who was five years younger, and in the spring of 1886, they were married.

Soon after the marriage they took a house on Brooklyn street, Halliwell, and for a while they lived happily together until disaster struck.

Walter lost his job at the mill and found it difficult to find alternative employment. He was surviving on club money of ten shillings a week, but this didn't go far for the family of four. Emma's wage didn't bring a great deal of money in and after a few weeks, she decided she had had enough and returned to live with her mother in Bury. Not only did she leave Walter a blunt note informing him of her intentions, but she also gathered together items of furniture and was gone when he returned from a day's job hunting.

Wood was devastated at the news and immediately pleaded for her to return, and began bombarding her with notes declaring his love. In desperation he travelled to Bury and confronted her on the door step. "Emma you are my wife, and if you don't come home soon I will kill you!". "You kill me and you'll be sure to hang!" she mocked, and then added seriously: "I will come back to live with you again, if you find work and settle down, but not before".

Realising that she was deadly serious, he vowed to win her back and returned to Bolton. On February 17th, 1887, he struck lucky. Carrying glowing testimonies from a former employer he called at a Bolton engineering works and secured a position for himself. His joy was short-lived however, for when he returned to his mother's house on Thynne street, there was a letter waiting for him.

Opening it up, he cursed at the contents and thrusting it into his jacket pocket, he stormed out of the house. Reaching Bury, he called at Emma's mother's house, but was unable to speak to his wife. He wrote a short note which he gave to a neighbour's child and asked her to deliver it. The note said that he had found work and requested that his wife meet him at Fitton's beer-house on nearby Walmsley road.

A short time later he was joined by his wife and they set out for a walk, passing through some adjacent fields. What transpired during the walk was never fully established, but a short time later a witness saw Emma running down a foot path towards Huntley Fold Farm with blood streaming from a gash to her neck.

"My husband has cut my throat", she cried before collapsing. The wound stretched from ear to ear and within a matter of minutes she had breathed her last. Police launched a hunt for Walter Wood but he had vanished. Officers kept a look-out at all nearby railway stations and at Liverpool docks as it was thought that he might try to make for America.

Wood went to ground for two days before he tried to make

a secret, late night, visit to his mother's house. Police, tipped off by a neighbour, hurried to the the house and arrested him for murder.

The officers escorted Wood back to Bury police station but as they approached the concourse they found an angry mob waiting and only quick thinking by a sergeant prevented Wood being lynched.

At his trial at Manchester Assizes, Wood pleaded not guilty to murder but guilty to the lesser charge of manslaughter in the hope of avoiding the gal-

Walter Wood.

lows. The judge's summing up however, left the jury and packed court in no doubt what verdict he believed to be the right one, and after just six minutes the jury returned and found him guilty of murder.

While awaiting the hangman, Wood confided in a relative that Emma had disclosed that she was pregnant shortly before he had cut her throat, a crime he had committed in a fit of uncontrolled passion.

On the afternoon of May 29th, hangman James Berry travelled to the prison from his home in Bradford. It was usual for the hangman to view the prisoner during exercise prior to rigging the scaffold, so he could get an idea of the drop needed for a correct execution. Spying the prisoner, Berry recognised him as a former classmate; the two attended school at

Wrea Green near Blackpool. Wood asked the hangman if he would sit with him for a while on the eve of the execution and Berry obliged.

Next morning on the stroke of eight, Walter Wood was led to the scaffold. As Berry placed the noose around his neck, the prisoner cried out "Lord have mercy on me". Moments later he was dead.

TERRIBLE MURDER NEAR BURY.

SHOCKING SCENE AFTER THE CRIME.

ESCAPE OF THE MURDERER.

Yesterday a shocking wife murder occurred at Bury, the deed being committed in a determined manner in broad daylight in a not very unfrequented place. The name of the murderer is Walter Wood, a machine fitter, who has been employed for some time at Asa Lees and Co.'s, Oldham, and more recently at Messrs. Dobson and

---

CHAPTER 21

The Body in the Wardrobe

THROUGHOUT the last month George Gordon, the area manager for his father's Manchester based furniture suppliers, had forsaken his weekly visit to the Bury branch as he was expecting to do business with a wealthy customer at the firm's main branch on Great Dulcie Street, Manchester. And for the last four weeks the wealthy customer, a Mr Alstead, had failed to keep the appointment which was always made for a Tuesday. On the fifth none showing Gordon began to suspect it was a ploy to keep him away from the Bury shop. With some justification.

The Bury branch was run by twenty eight year old William Dukes. Although he lived happily with his wife and young family in Bolton, Dukes was a womaniser and a client to several local prostitutes, whose favours he paid for with small items of furniture from the shop, items which he failed to account for and which were now beginning to appear as stock short falls.

Tuesday was the day on which Mr Gordon usually visited the Bury shop to check the accounts and on his last visit at the end of August 1889, he told Dukes that their were discrepancies amongst the stock and that he had better have sorted it out before his next visit or he would be in serious trouble.

George Gordon.

Dukes decided on a scheme to stall Gordon's visits but realising that this could only ever be a temporary measure and that sooner or later he would receive a visit.

On Wednesday morning, September 25th, 1889, the shop was opened by nineteen year old William Tootill, Dukes's junior. Although he was an ambitious man who suspected that the manager was fiddling the books, and knowing that a word in the right ear from him could see him promoted into Dukes's shoes, he was nonetheless an honourable man and also fond of the sometimes easy going Dukes.

At 9-30am that morning, George Gordon finally managed to call at the shop to see the manager. Dukes, who had spotted Gordon's approach, slipped out of the back door and took sanctuary in the adjacent public house while he put into action another plan.

At 11-45am, he arranged for a telegram to be delivered to the Bury shop telling Tootill that if Mr Gordon calls to tell him he is at the Manchester branch with a client, Mr Alstead. Alstead had ordered a number of items to be despatched to him from the Bury shop later that afternoon.

Dukes returned to the shop shortly after lunch ready for the inevitable showdown. Gordon asked Dukes to show him the accounts and the two headed off to the warehouse at the back of the shop.

At shortly after 2 o'clock, George Fowler, a warehouseman from the Manchester branch arrived by cart to collect the customer order for Mr Alstead destined for Lime Tree House, Prestwich. Arriving at the warehouse door, Fowler stumbled in on a heated argument between the manager and area manager, and creeping away unseen he told William Tootill what he had heard. "Well, he's had it coming" Tootill simply said of his boss.

At 2-45pm, Gordon and Dukes entered the courtyard to watch over the cart being loaded up with Mr Alstead's order and at 3pm Dukes handed Tootill and Fowler a note saying that Mr Gordon and Mr Alstead had caught the train to Prestwich and they had better be quick with the delivery if they didn't want to incur Gordon's wrath. The two young men set out for Prestwich, but despite searching for over an hour they couldn't find any Lime Tree House and reluctantly the cart returned to Bury fully ladened.

Dukes scolded the two and said that he would take it himself tomorrow, then walked off towards the pub. Deciding not to leave the cart fully loaded overnight, Tootill emptied it and tried to put the goods back in the warehouse but found it locked. This angered him as it meant he must wait with the goods until Dukes returned, but fortunately he was only away a few minutes.

Unlocking the warehouse door, Dukes told Fowler to return to Manchester and

William Dukes.

93

that if old Sam (George's father and head of the firm) asked where George is, to tell him he had gone to the Burnley shop. Tootill and Fowler looked across at each other aware that only a couple of hours earlier Dukes had told them Gordon had accompanied the customer to Prestwich. Even more surprisingly Dukes then told them that they could finish early that night as he intended to visit the theatre in Manchester.

At 11 o'clock next morning, Sam Gordon and his son Meyer called at the shop anxious about the whereabouts of George Gordon who had been missing since the previous morning. Both knew that George was having problems with the manager who he suspected was 'cooking the books' and they decided to confront him face to face.

"Where's George?", Meyer demanded.

"He went to the Burnley shop", Dukes told him.

"Nonsense!", he shouted, "Do you know what day it was yesterday?"

Dukes shook his head as Meyer continued.

"At sunset yesterday we celebrated the Jewish New Year. George would not dream of being away from his family on this day. And anyway the Burnley shop has closed for the holidays."

Dukes tried to offer an explanation but Meyer told him he could say what he had to say to the police and grabbed him by the arm. Dukes allowed himself to be taken to the local police station, where Gordon relayed his suspicions to the desk sergeant.

Officers accompanied them back to the warehouse and searched it. They were immediately attracted to the scene in one of the rooms which looked as if a fight had taken place there. Furniture was knocked over and on a table lay a bloodstained screwdriver.

Superintendent Henderson pointed to a door in the corner and asked what was down there. "Oh, it's only a cellar, there's nothing much down there" Dukes said not too confidently. Deciding to take a look for themselves, the search party descended the staircase and lit up the room with their lanterns. One policeman noticed some ashes in the grate and a closer look showed them to be the shops accounts. A search of a dark corner found a number of flagstones raised and a shallow trench had begun to take shape, as if someone was preparing a grave.

It seemed likely in the circumstances that the grave was intended for the missing man, but he clearly wasn't there.

"Where is my brother?" Meyer shouted at Dukes who remained silent. On the other side of the room was a large wardrobe. Old man Gordon asked who it belonged to and Dukes told him it was for a customer in Rochdale. Meyer went to lift it and found it very heavy. "It's full of books and some smaller items", Dukes told him.

THE

TERRIBLE MURDER

OF A

MANCHESTER MAN

AT BURY.

Our own reporter telegraphing to-day says :—The sensation created in Bury yesterday by the news of the shocking discovery in Bolton-street has been intensified as the details of the ghastly tragedy have come to be known.

The branch shop of the "Gordon Furnishing Company" in which the murder has been committed is situated in Bolton-street, about a hundred yards from the Bolton-street railway station. It is a building of two storeys and attic, and has been in the possession of the "Gordon Furnishing Company" since the branch in Bury was opened, three or four years ago. Some time after the branch was opened the firm—which consisted of Samuel Gordon and his two sons, Meyers and George—

The police officer asked for the key and was told that the customer had the only one. Meyer picked up a screwdriver from the workbench and put it against the lock. Dukes made an effort to intervene but was restrained and was forced to watch in silence as the lock was prised open. Inside the wardrobe was the battered body of George Gordon. Dukes was placed under arrest and when searched was found to have the key concealed in his waistcoat pocket.

Six weeks later Dukes stood trial before Mr Justice Charles at Manchester Assizes. He pleaded not guilty and told the court his version of the events regarding the death of George Gordon.

He said that there had been an argument at the shop, whereupon Gordon had threatened to punch him. Dukes told him that he could dismiss him if he wanted to but he had no right to hit him. He then claimed that Gordon picked up a hammer and rushed towards him. He threw him off and as he did so Gordon slipped and struck his head on the fireplace.

Dukes then claimed that he then panicked and decided to bury the body in a shallow grave in the cellar. His defence counsel concluded by asking for a verdict of manslaughter.

The prosecution contested this theory on several points but the two main pointers were that a doctor had confirmed cause of death as by a hammer blow, and a hammer was found beside the body in the wardrobe. The second was the elaborate plan Dukes had set to throw them off the trail parts of which had been put into action long before Gordons death which showed that his death wasn't the result of a spur of the moment quarrel, more likely the work of a callous calculated killer. The jury agreed and found him guilty of murder.

On Christmas eve he was hanged at Strangeways prison by James Berry, the law decreeing that he should meet his fate on the eve of a Christian celebration, just as his victim had met his on the eve of the Jewish New year.

CHAPTER 22

The Atherton Pawnshop Murder

IT was a lovely summer's morning as twenty one year old Walter Davies left his home on Mealhouse lane, Atherton, and walked the short distance to work. He may have smiled as he thought how in just a few short weeks he was to marry his sweetheart.

He reached the small pawn brokers shop on Market street, where he worked as the assistant manager at shortly before 8 o'clock, Monday, July 22nd, 1889, and after opening the shop, his first task was to restock the window with the more expensive items that had been kept in the safe over the weekend.

At a few minutes to nine, a friend called into the shop hoping for a chat, but seeing Walter talking to a customers, he said 'hello' and told him he would call back later.

Five minutes later, a neighbouring shop-keeper called into the shop for some change and found it apparently deserted. She called out and heard no reply. Becoming alarmed, she crossed over to the wicket gate in the counter and as she did so she heard a faint moaning coming from the cellar. Walking behind the counter she saw the trap door was raised, and look-

Walter Davies.

ing down she saw Walter lying in a pool of blood. He had a vicious wound to the temple and his throat had been cut.

She hurried to fetch the police but before officers could reach the scene, Walter Davies had died.

It was soon clear why Walter had been killed. The window display of watches and broaches had been cleared out, as had the contents of the till, and Walter's own watch and chain.

Detectives reasoned that the killer would try to pass on the stolen goods, probably through alternative pawnshops, and this theory was proved correct when goods were recovered from various shops as far afield as Liverpool and Stockport. The items recovered included Walter's own watch, but despite offering a reward police were unable to build up a picture of the wanted man.

Initially, all available officers were assigned to the case but as the weeks dragged by the hunt was gradually scaled down. A number of suspects were questioned, and one man in particular was held for several weeks until his innocence could be proven.

Amongst other enquiries the Lancashire police were investigating, were a series of thefts from railway wagons at Patricroft and Eccles and after a tip-off a man was arrested in connection with these thefts.

Identified as William Matthew Chadwick, a twenty-three year old Manchester man, Chadwick soon aroused suspicion that he may be involved in the Atherton murder when he told a police officer questioning him, that he expected to be charged with a more serious crime than handling stolen property.

The police had recently taken possession of a camera and officers took a photograph of Chadwick and took it to several of the pawn shops were goods had been retrieved from the Atherton shop. It was an astute move. Several shop-keepers claimed that the picture closely resembled the seller and satisfied that Chadwick was their man, detectives charged him with the murder.

His trial was held at Liverpool Assizes in the spring of 1890. The defence claimed that the case against Chadwick was flimsy to say the least and that the only evidence was circumstantial. The prosecution had no witnesses to the crime nor was there any evidence linking Chadwick to the scene of the crime. Chadwick, they claimed, was being held solely on the evidence of a photograph.

For their part the prosecution admitted that much of the evidence was merely circumstantial but many witnesses were prepared to swear that Chadwick had sold them items which were proved to have come from the Atherton shop, and to further support this the names signed in the register were all former aliases of the prisoner.

All told, the prosecution called seventy witnesses, and despite Chadwick vehement denials in the dock, the jury were convinced of his guilt and need only a

WILLIAM CHADWICK.

The Police photograph of Chadwick.

99

The Pawn Broker's shop on Market Street, Atherton, where Walter Davies was brutally murdered.

short time to find him guilty of murder. Mr Justice Mathew passed sentence of death on the prisoner who shouted that he was innocent and not afraid to die as he was ushered from the dock.

From the condemned cell Chadwick protested his innocence to such a degree that any members of his family who had doubted his innocence, rapidly changed their minds and gave their full support to the petitions for a reprieve.

Unswayed by the protests, the Home Secretary refused to

sanction a reprieve, and on April 15th, he was hanged at Kirkdale by James Berry.

POSTSCIPT: Chadwick was certainly a thief, of that there was no doubt, but was he a murderer? It is true to say that the police use of the photograph was the main pointer in the case, but just as damning was the fact that the names signed in the pledge books were all names assumed at one time or another by Chadwick, and the fact that the one shopkeeper who was adamant that Chadwick had sold him the stolen goods was the one who had purchased Walter Davies's watch and chain, just hours after it had been brutally stolen from him.

CHAPTER 23

The Belmont School Teacher Murder

ARLY on the morning of Monday, November 10th, 1890, twenty-one year old Miss Elizabeth Holt set out from her home in Dunscar to walk the three or so miles to Belmont, where she was a teacher at the village school. She never arrived.

During school term Elizabeth divided her time between her widowed mother's house and lodging with a fellow school master and his family. When she failed to arrive at school, she was thought to be sick, and with her not expected home until the weekend she wasn't missed by her family. Indeed, it wasn't until late Friday night that her sister began to worry that something was amiss. She re-assured her mother that Lizzie must have stayed late at school and, with the winter nights drawing in, had decided to wait until morning before walking home.

On the following Saturday morning a young lad out walking his dog in Longworth Clough came across the body of his school-teacher. She had been battered about the head, her throat had been savagely ripped open and her clothing was torn.

Miss Elizabeth Holt.

Police hurried to the scene and led by Sergeant Hayward they arranged for the body to be moved to her mother's cottage were it was later examined by Doctor Robinson. The doctor was able to say that in his opinion Miss Holt had been dead for approximately a week and that she had died from her head and throat injuries.

Police were at a loss as to the motive, as Lizzie was a popular lass, well liked and respected in the village, and had been neither robbed nor raped.

Investigations in the nearby area soon turned up a vital clue. Farmer Robert Scholes remembered that he had been delivering milk on Monday morning when he spotted Lizzie walking along Longworth Lane, close to the clough. He told officers that following the teacher down the lane, at a distance behind, was Thomas McDonald.

Thirty-two year old McDonald was well known to the police as a local ruffian, and was still in the frame as the likely killer of a young navvy who had been drowned in a local mill pond a few weeks earlier. They had arrested McDonald almost at once but had been forced to release him as finding any conclusive evidence, other than strong suspicion, was not forthcoming. He also had a prison record for assault on a young woman.

Later that Saturday afternoon McDonald was visited by Sergeant Hayward and Constables Hargreaves and Johnstone. He was staying with his aunt in Egerton and when he opened the

door he was told he was
being taken in for questioning regarding the murder of
Elizabeth Ann Holt at Longworth Clough.

THE PRISONER.
FROM A SKETCH TAKEN IN COURT.

Instead of making an out-
right denial, McDonald
readily admitted being in
the area at the time but
claimed that he was merely
making his way to Long-
worth Colliery where he
spent the day working as a
casual labourer. He also admitted that after getting
paid that evening he got
drunk and had been ar-
rested for being drunk and
disorderly.

An initial check of his statement proved that some of it was
correct, at least the part about being arrested was. The arrest-
ing officer also confirmed that McDonald's clothing was heavily blood-stained, which the prisoner claimed was the result of
a fight. Knowing the sort of person McDonald was there was
no reason to suspect he wasn't telling the truth about the
blood.

The evidence needed to break the alibi was supplied by
John Brierly, the manager at Longworth Colliery. He admitted
employing McDonald on several occasions but was adamant
that Monday, November 10th, wasn't one of those days.

A forensic officer from Liverpool examined his clothing and
found traces of blood but police knew any defence lawyer
could explain these away.

As police investigations progressed, the funeral of the murdered teacher took place. The country was still living in the

shadow of the 'Jack the Ripper' murders in London's White-chapel, and one national newspaper compared the Belmont atrocity as 'as barbaric as the work of the Ripper'.

The vital proof needed to charge McDonald with murder was supplied by his aunt, Mrs Honor Bann. The long suffering aunt, a devout catholic, had covered for him on lesser charges before, but her conscience wouldn't allow her on this occasion and she told police that McDonald had confessed to her that he had killed the young teacher. When police told him of his aunt's statement, McDonald's head sank into his chest and he made a full confession.

On December 13th, Thomas McDonald was tried for his crime at Liverpool Assizes before Mr Justice Cave. He pleaded not guilty to the charge. The crown prosecutor put forward a strong case of convincing the packed court that McDonald was guilty. Evidence was heard from a number of witnesses but the most dramatic moment came when McDonald's confession was read out:

"At 8 o'clock on the morning of November 10th, I started from home to go over to Belmont to see the manager of Longworth Collieries about work. On Longworth Lane I overtook the deceased. As soon as I overtook her, I got hold of her shoulder. I asked her what she had been telling lies about me for. I told her that she had set it out that I'd followed her a few weeks ago for the purpose of doing her harm. She told me to let go of her shoulder. I told her I would not do so until she had retracted what she had said. She jerked her shoulder away out of my hand, shut her umbrella, took hold of the small end of it and struck me with it. I became enraged, threw her down and beat her about the head and cut her throat.

Then I dragged her across the lane and threw her into Longworth Clough. I cut open her clothes to see if her heart was still beating. I found it did not beat. I then went home".

"A great many people think this girl was got hold of for

105

the purpose of ravishing her, but I can swear on my dying oath such is not the case".

The prosecution then told the court of a second statement made twenty-four hours later in which he added more details of the murder:

"Man, I had a job with her. When she struck me with the umbrella on the head, she might have got away, for I was quiet for a few minutes. The first time I knocked her down she got up and I had to put my leg behind hers before I got her down a second time. I soon finished her off then with my clogs and the knife. When I took her to the bottom of the clough I was nearly making a mess of myself. When I was half way home I was looking for my knife to cut some tobacco. I had to go back for it, and when I went back for it I found it underneath the body".

In the face of such damning testimonies, McDonald's defence made a dramatic plea for the prisoners life. "There is no doubt he is guilty of a cruel and violent homicide, but I plead not for an acquittal, not for the establishment of his innocence, I plead for his life alone.

Suddenly, without warning, McDonald jumped to his feet and shouted "I don't want it. I am guilty, let it drop". The jury took less than an hour to find the prisoner guilty as charged and the Judge condemned him to death.

At 8am, on new years eve 1890, at Kirkdale prison, Liverpool, Thomas McDonald kept a final appointment with hangman James Berry.

CHAPTER 24

The Hangman's Friend

ON a warm Monday afternoon, the end of September 1901, Mrs Ann McKenna, heavily laden with the weeks shopping, and tired from the up-hill walk home, turned into Kestor Street, a row of bleak terrace houses in the quiet residential area of the Haulgh, Bolton.

She lived at number five with her husband, Pat, and shared the house with two lodgers, Mr and Mrs Palmer. Ann chose not to go straight home, heading instead for her son's house, six doors away on the same cobbled street, where she could rest her weary feet over a cup of tea with her daughter-in-law, Emily.

Ann had scarcely put the shopping down when her husband entered the house. Patrick McKenna, was a fifty-three year old former joiner who, since losing his job earlier that year, had only been able to find casual work as a labourer and, depressed at being unable to find a better paid skilled job, he had taken to drinking heavily.

Since finishing his shift on Saturday lunchtime, McKenna had been drinking constantly, and it was from the vault of the local pub that he had spotted his wife returning home. He knew she had called at a pawn shop and began to demand money for more drink.

Ann was reluctant to part with the paltry sum she had col-

107

lected from pawning some jewellery, especially as it was only to spend on drink. In no uncertain terms she told him he wasn't having a penny, adding: "If you want to waste money on drink, you must go to work and earn it".

Patrick McKenna.

In a rage McKenna stormed from the house, cursing as he left that he would "cut her throat before the day was through". It was a threat he had made many times before. Watching him leave, Ann and Emily settled down to drink their tea and gossip.

McKenna had been gone barely five minutes, when he returned. This time his approach was different. He pleaded for enough for one drink, but Ann was adamant and told him he wasn't having anything. He stormed out again and this time Emily locked the front door. Five minutes later he returned and unable to gain entry, began banging on the door. Emily shouted at him through the window, "she's gone to see your Mary".

He called at his daughter Mary's house, a few streets away, and when no-one answered he stormed back to Kestor street, determined to seek out his wife. She wasn't at home so he returned to his son's house and again pounded on the door. Emily repeated that his wife was no longer here and he snapped: "perhaps she's in bed with Palmer", referring to his lodger who he suspected was having an affair with his wife.

In reality, Ann had hiding in the kitchen and would have escaped her husband's pestering if he hadn't decided to try to enter the house by the back door. As he opened the gate he spotted his wife through the window and stormed in, before either Ann or Emily could fasten the latch.

McKenna demanded to know where she had been, and accused her of being too familiar with Palmer. Emily told him not to be so stupid, but Ann had underestimated the degree of his rage, for when she scoffed at him he picked up a carving knife off the table and plunged it deep into her neck.

Alerted by a scream, neighbours rushed into the house and found Ann McKenna lying mortally wounded in the floor. A number of the men tried to detain McKenna who had gone berserk, and eventually, after a struggle, they managed to force him into a neighbours coal-cellar, holding it shut until the police arrived.

Police Constable Spencer was first to the scene. He saw that Mrs McKenna was beyond help and after summoning a taxi, escorted McKenna to the police station. When the prisoner sobered up he apologised and made a full statement admitting the crime.

On Wednesday, November 13th, 1901, Patrick McKenna stood in the dock at Manchester Assizes. Mr Justice Bucknill presided. Before the first witness was called, the Judge ordered the court to be cleared of the many young children who crowded in the gallery, adding that a court was not a fit place for them and that he was also saddened to see so many women present.

McKenna pleaded not guilty to the charge of wilful murder but there was little doubt as to what the outcome of the trial would be. His counsel took the only option open to them and offered a plea of insanity; claiming there was hereditary madness in the family, and that McKenna's brother had been confined to an asylum.

The prosecution claimed that it was simply a brutal murder fuelled by drink and jealousy and that he deserved the full penalty of the law. The jury agreed and took only twenty-nine minutes to find him guilty. Mr Justice Bucknill then donned the black cap and sentenced the sad looking man to death.

The execution was fixed for December 3rd at Strangeways prison, Manchester. The country's chief hangman was still James Billington, the landlord of the Derby Arms, on Church-gate, Bolton, one of McKenna's regular haunts, and both men were well known to each other having grown up on the same street.

There was also another link between the prisoner and the hangman, for one of the men who had tended the stricken Mrs McKenna, and helped detain her killer, was William "Billy" Billington, the executioner's son, and also a hangman. Billy wasn't involved in this particular job as the assistant chosen was Henry Pierrepoint, the first of that family of famous hangmen.

EXECUTION OF THE BOLTON MURDERER.

Within the walls of Strangeways Gaol, Manchester, at eight o'clock, on Tuesday morning, Patrick McKenna, of 5, Kestor-st., Bolton, was executed for the murder of his wife on the 30th of September last. As our readers are aware the Rev. W. Fowler, of St. Mary's Roman Catholic Church, Palace-st., with other friends, had interested himself in the case, and had done his utmost to avert, if possible, the carrying out of the last dread sentence of the law by endeavouring to obtain a reprieve for the condemned man, and a petition, signed by no fewer than 22,500 persons, was presented to the Home

It was customary for the hangmen to arrive at the prison by sunset on the day before the execution and remain inside until their duties were over. On the night before, after preparing the equipment for the morning, Billington, who had left his sick bed to attend, was taken ill and Pierrepoint offered to carry out the job for him. The hangmen declined the offer saying that he wanted to see it through.

On the stroke of eight next morning, the two executioners entered the cell and found McKenna crying bitterly. They secured his arms and led the sobbing and distraught man across the corridor to the gallows. As Billington adjusted the noose, McKenna cried out "Lord have mercy on me". Seconds later the floor crashed down and the rope jerked tight; McKenna had paid for his crime.

Later that morning the hangmen parted at Manchester's Victoria Station. Billington was in a bad way and had to be helped into his carriage by his assistant. His last words to Pierrepoint were "Harry, I wish I'd never have come". Ten days later he died from pneumonia, brought on, his friends said, by leaving his sick-bed to hang his old friend.